JOURNEY TO THE JUSTICE LEAGUE

From the warrior princess of Themyscira to Gotham's Dark Knight, and a powerful, selfless Kryptonian, Super Heroes have been emerging on Earth... We trace the story – so far – of the Justice League's world...

Feature by Jonathan Wilkins

WONDER WOMAN

On the island of Themyscira live the Amazons, a powerful all-female race created by Zeus to defend humanity.

In 1918, a plane crashed into the sea off the coast of Themyscira. Diana rescued the pilot, American spy Steve Trevor. He told the Amazons of a "War to End All Wars" in Europe and of his mission to return home with information about a deadly strain of gas being developed under the command of General Erich Ludendorff. Convinced that Ludendorff was Ares, the God of War, Diana escorted Steve back to the Supreme War Council in England where they met Sir Patrick Morgan, who was trying to negotiate an armistice with Germany.

Diana led a squad deep behind enemy lines and killed Ludendorff, but was shocked to discover that Sir Patrick was actually Ares… Their final battle saw Steve valiantly sacrifice his own life to destroy the gas bombs while Diana killed Ares.

MAN OF STEEL

Rocketed to Earth, as a baby, from the doomed planet Krypton, Kal-El was raised as the adopted son of Jonathan and Martha Kent in Smallville, Kansas, and named Clark.

Years later, Clark found a buried Kryptonian spaceship in the Canadian Arctic and learned of his true origin and purpose, to inspire and protect humanity. Donning a suit left by his Kryptonian father, Clark introduced himself to the world as Superman.

A Kryptonian general named Zod gave Superman an ultimatum, join him or die. Zod proceeded to terraform the Earth, transforming it into a new Krypton. However, the Man of Steel was able to destroy Zod's terraformer, The World Engine. In a final confrontation, Superman was forced to kill Zod.

Appalled by the carnage caused by the battle, Bruce Wayne, secretly the Batman, vowed to never let this happen again…

EDITOR'S NOTE

As a little kid, comics soon became a huge part of my life, and most of my pocket money was spent on them. My first *Justice League* comics were in the Justice League Detroit era (I'll always have a soft spot for that team – ah, Gypsy!), where the team met a tragic end. Luckily, the team soon bounced back in *Legends*, *Justice League International*, and Grant Morrison's *JLA* series.

It's weird, now, to think that the Super Hero comics I read back in those days – all alone in a corner of the living room on my beanbag! – are now the subjects of these big, blockbuster movies that everyone gets all excited about!

The *Justice League* movie brings a new element to the DC movie universe – that of teamwork. Fittingly, everything about *Justice League The Official Collector's Edition* has been a team effort. The support and input from Warner Bros. and the movie's producers has been extraordinary, and it was quite a thrill to have regular conference calls with them (yes, I did get a little

starstruck). And the support from my colleagues has also been phenomenal. When I was knee-deep in writing or proofreading, there was always someone willing to help with biography writing or picture research.

So what have we got in store for you over the next 95 pages? Well, I'm delighted to tell you that we've got pretty much everything. All of the main cast are interviewed, plus we have really cool interviews with some of the supporting actors. We have a huge behind-the-scenes section, kicking off with an interview with some of the producers (where they reveal some of the film's secrets), we have a special insight into the creation of the all-important costumes, plus we delve deep into the designs for the worlds and characters of Aquaman, Cyborg, and The Flash – and all of these features are stunningly illustrated with absolutely gorgeous images. And there's lots more, too!

But anyway, that's enough from me – I'll let you check it out for yourselves. Enjoy!

Martin Eden
Editor, *Justice League The Official Collector's Edition*

EDITORIAL
Senior Editor **Martin Eden**
Senior Designer **Andrew Leung**
Contributors **David Leach, Jonathan Wilkins,**
Nick Jones, Jonathan Stevenson
Thank you to **Thank you to Amy Weingartner,**
Alisha Stevens, Josh Anderson, Charles Roven,
Deborah Snyder, Zack Snyder, Geoff Johns,
Jon Berg, Wesley Coller, Curtis Kanemoto,
Madison Weireter, Adam Schlagman, Galen
Vaisman, Shane Thompson, Spencer Douglas,
and all of the cast and crew of the JL movie for
giving up their valuable time to help with this
publication. Thanks also to Michael Wilkinson

Patrick Tatopoulos, Clay Enos, Eren Ramadan,
Tony Barbera, Leah Tuttle, Mike Pallotta, and
Doug Prinzivalli, and all the *Justice League*
team at Warner Bros.
Editorial Assistant **Tolly Maggs**
Art Director **Oz Browne**
Advertising and Marketing Assistant **Tom Miller**
Direct Sales & Marketing Manager **Ricky Claydon**
Senior Sales Manager **Steve Tothill**
Commercial Manager **Michelle Fairlamb**
Production Controller **Peter James**
Production Supervisor **Maria James**
Senior Production Controller **Jackie Flook**
Publishing Manager **Darryl Tothill**

Publishing Director **Chris Teather**
Executive Director **Vivian Cheung**
Publisher **Nick Landau**
DISTRIBUTION
US Newsstand: Total Publisher Services, Inc.
John Dziewiatkowski, 630-851-7693; US
Distribution: Ingram Periodicals, Curtis Circulation
Company; UK Newsstand: Marketforce, 0203
7879199; UK Direct Sales Market: Diamond
Comic Distributors.

Justice League The Official Collector's Edition,
2017, published by Titan Magazines, a division
of Titan Publishing Group, 144 Southwark Street,
London, SE1 0UP TCN: 13607

CONTENTS

BATMAN V SUPERMAN

While the LexCorp company helped to reconstruct Metropolis following General Zod and Superman's fight, its CEO, Lex Luthor, discovered Kryptonite from Zod's downed World Engine. He also gained access to Zod's remains and the Kryptonian scout ship in Metropolis. Elsewhere, Bruce Wayne met Clark Kent and Diana Prince at a gala at Luthor's estate where Wayne was attempting to retrieve encrypted data from Lex's computer system, which later revealed that

Luthor had been investigating metahumans, including Arthur Curry: Aquaman, Victor Stone: Cyborg, Barry Allen: The Flash, and Diana Prince: Wonder Woman.

Fearing the worst, Batman created an armored mech suit and stole Luthor's Kryptonite to forge a powerful spear should he ever have to fight Superman.

Luthor kidnapped Martha Kent, and forced Superman to fight Batman for her safe return. The two heroes launched into a brutal

combat, which Batman narrowly won, although he stopped short of killing Superman when he learned he had been forced to fight by Luthor. Batman raced to save Martha, while Luthor unleashed a monstrous creature, Doomsday (born of the mutated DNA of Zod), on the city. Only the surprise intervention of Wonder Woman saved the day when she joined forces with Batman and Superman to fight the seemingly unstoppable creature.

Superman killed the monster using the Kryptonite spear, but with its dying breath Doomsday killed Superman.

Realizing that the Man of Steel's death had left the world undefended from powerful alien threats, Bruce became inspired by Superman's selfless act. He revealed to Diana his plan to form a team of metahumans, starting with those from Luthor's files, to help protect the world from an oncoming unknown threat.

BEN AFFLECK IS
BATMAN

Ben Affleck once again dons the cape and body armor of Gotham City's greatest vigilante, Batman, in *Justice League*. Here, Affleck reveals how Bruce Wayne dealt with the aftermath of Superman's sacrifice, which led him to form a mighty league of Super Heroes...

Justice League Collector's Edition: What's been happening to Bruce Wayne since we left him at the end of *Batman v Superman*?

Ben Affleck: Bruce was feeling fearful at the end of that movie from Luthor's warning that a bell had been rung. He was worrying that there was some kind of attack coming, so he's decided to gather together as many metahumans as he possibly can. Where we left things, he was in the nascent stages of building a team – he was starting to research. This movie begins with Bruce trying to find these superhumans that he believes are out there. He is actively recruiting.

Some of them are more willing to come along than others. What different reactions does he get when he starts tracking people down?

He's not met with enthusiasm by everybody that he encounters. Some people are a little bit more reluctant to join up and become part of the team. The Flash signs right up, but Aquaman takes some convincing. Wonder Woman

Ben Affleck all suited up as the Dark Knight

BIO

Born in Berkeley, California, **Ben Affleck** is an actor, director, and writer with two Academy Awards, three Golden Globes, two BAFTAs, and two Screen Actor Guild awards to his credit. His acting career started in 1981 when he appeared in an independent film called *The Dark End of the Street*. He went on to appear in cult classics such as *Dazed and Confused* and Kevin Smith's *Chasing Amy* and *Mallrats*. In 1997, Affleck and Matt Damon won a Golden Globe and Academy Award for Best Original Screenplay for the film *Good Will Hunting*, which they also starred in. Affleck cemented his status as a leading man in *Armageddon* and *Pearl Harbor* before winning his second Golden Globe and Academy Award for Best Picture in 2012 for the film *Argo*. In 2016, he starred as Batman in both *Batman v Superman* and *Suicide Squad*.

steps in to bring Cyborg around, and eventually they all realize that there's a need for them to work together, and they collectively start to assemble this group.

What compels Wonder Woman and Batman to work together?

It goes back to the funeral scene in *Batman v Superman*, where Bruce tells Diana, "We're going to need to work together. We're going to need to find the others." I think she's a little bit skeptical, but once she sees a symbol only Amazons would recognize for an active invasion, she quickly steps up and contributes to the recruiting effort.

For people who don't follow the comics, can you explain what a "Mother Box" is?

A Mother Box is an all-powerful, indestructible, technological cube that can also teleport a bunch of aliens to Earth from another world.

And bringing three Mother Boxes together is not a good thing, right?

Once you combine the three Mother Boxes they form what's called the Unity, a force that is pure power used to conquer worlds.

Fortunately, these things don't exist in real life, of course, but they're a part of the DC Universe, and a problem for the Justice League.

A big part of the Batman mythos is his bag of tricks. What's new in the armory this time? ▶

01

02

03

▶ Bruce Wayne has no shortage of ways to get around. He's got a new futuristic civilian vehicle, the Mercedes-Benz AMG Vision Gran Turismo, which is only fit for someone of Bruce Wayne's stature. Then there's the newly modified Batmobile, which gets tricked out to take on the unknown threat, making it just that little bit more lethal. Bruce also has his huge commercial jet that he flies around whenever he needs to be transported somewhere. And he's building an even bigger troop carrier for when he wants to go longer distances into battle.

The Batsuits are getting an upgrade too, like the mean-looking tactical suit.
Yes, I wear the tactical suit when we have to get more serious and more deadly. It's more armored, more tricked out, and cooler. I'm sure it'll make a great action figure.

How was it shooting the scene when the whole JL finally comes together in full costumes?
It's fun to see all the other Justice League characters in their costumes, so you don't feel like the only guy in tights! But other than that, it's pretty surreal when you have Aquaman, Wonder Woman, Flash, Superman, and Batman all dressed up. You feel a little bit less like you're performing at a kid's birthday party and more like you're making a pretty cool movie. And it's really impressive to see the work and the energy that went into the aesthetic of these costumes.

Ray Fisher doesn't really have a costume as Cyborg, it's all CGI and added in post-production, so he was just wearing pajamas.

With so much use of green screen on every set, how hard is it for you to stay focused?
Everything's imaginary. You have to imagine that all these things

> **"BATMAN'S TACTICAL SUIT IS SERIOUS AND DEADLY. IT'S MORE ARMORED AND IT'S COOLER. IT'LL MAKE A GREAT ACTION FIGURE!"**

are happening around you, and the temptation is to stop paying attention. It's hard to get your energy up and stay motivated, to try to hold all these things in your imagination when virtually everything is going be put in later by a computer.

You'd prefer to be taking the Batmobile out to a racetrack, then?
Yes! Now that would be fun. Drag racing the Batmobile – that's

the kind of thing I like. That's the real thing.

What about Bruce's relationship with Alfred? Has that changed at all in this movie?
The Bruce/Alfred relationship continues in the same vein as in *Batman v Superman*. Alfred's a little bit sarcastic, a little bit sardonic, and gives Bruce an alternative perspective when he needs to hear it. He's the one who can let the air out of Bruce Wayne's balloon, and keep him grounded.

And now you've got J.K. Simmons playing Commissioner Jim Gordon. What's J.K.'s version of Commissioner Gordon like?
I did another movie with J.K. called *The Accountant*, and he's a fine actor. I really like him. Obviously he was great in *Whiplash*, and he's perfect as Commissioner Gordon. J.K. lends a real gravitas to the role. He's got that kind of realism down, where he's just so world weary and gritty.

EXECUTIVE ROLE

JL Collector's Edition: As an executive producer, you have a close involvement with where the DC Extended Universe is headed. What's exciting to you about the possibilities of that relationship? **Ben Affleck:** "It's fun to see storylines cross over and connect with one another. It's not something I've ever had a chance to do previously – this multiple-film connectivity thing. It's pretty cool, all the little Easter eggs that lead into each other."

It feels like here's a guy that's been working the beat of Gotham for decades.

He was pretty ripped in *The Accountant...*
I think he just likes to be ripped (*laughs*). It's a little weird, it's like the Super Hero Commissioner Gordon, who takes his shirt off and starts flexing (*laughs*)! J.K.'s just as strong as the members of the Justice League.

What's next for this story? What kind of adventures can we see the Justice League undertake next time out?
Now the Justice League is together, we have these stories that we can finally tell without being encumbered with setting up the backstory. We've done all that, so now we get to enjoy the adventures of this group of heroes as they take on the world. 🖐

THE COMIC BOOK ORIGINS OF...
BRUCE WAYNE – BATMAN

REAL NAME
BRUCE WAYNE

CREATED BY BOB KANE
WITH BILL FINGER

FIRST APPEARANCE
DETECTIVE COMICS #27
(MAY 1939)

**FIRST JOINED THE
LEAGUE** *BRAVE AND
THE BOLD* (VOL. 1) #28
(MARCH 1960)

POWERS AND ABILITIES
THE WORLD'S GREATEST
DETECTIVE, BATMAN'S
INTELLECT IS ALMOST
WITHOUT RIVAL. HIS
BODY TRAINED TO PEAK
PHYSICAL CONDITION. HE
IS A MASTER OF MARTIAL
ARTS AND HAND-TO-
HAND COMBAT, ABLE TO
CALL ON AN ARSENAL OF
NON-LETHAL WEAPONRY,
EQUIPMENT, AND VEHICLES.

He is Gotham City's defender, a Dark Knight waging a relentless – and frequently lonely – war on crime from the shadows. As such, Batman's relationship with the Justice League has sometimes been uneasy, but the team has come to rely on his fearsome intellect and tactical genius.

Batman debuted in comics in 1939 as a noirish counterpart to the more colorful Superman – very much a man as opposed to a superhuman, albeit one who had honed his mind and body to perfection. His origin tale in *Detective Comics* #33 (reprinted in the first issue of *Batman* in 1940) recounted how, as a boy, Bruce Wayne had witnessed his parents' murder at the hands of a

thief, and had sworn to avenge their deaths "by spending the rest of [his] life warring on all criminals." Accordingly, Bruce became a master scientist and also trained his body, but realized that he needed a disguise – one that would strike terror into the hearts of superstitious and cowardly criminals. As he pondered this dilemma, a bat flew in through his study window, inspiring Bruce to "become a bat!"

"And thus is born this weird figure of the dark" as that origin had it – although not as weird as the adversaries Batman would face: the most bizarre – and memorable – rogues gallery in comics, among their number the Joker, the Penguin, Two-Face, the

Riddler, Ra's al Ghul, Catwoman (on occasion), Poison Ivy, the Scarecrow, Harley Quinn, and, more recently, the Court of Owls. Even with the vast resources his inherited wealth provides him – an array of vehicles, planes, weaponry, and bases, most notably the Batcave beneath Wayne Manor – it was a small wonder that Batman soon took on a young partner in the shape of Robin, alias young circus performer Dick Grayson (later to become Nightwing).

Over the course of his comics career, Batman has endured trials, tribulations, and hardships that would have defeated most men: the death of the second Robin, Jason Todd (later resurrected); having his back broken (by super-villain Bane); being replaced as Batman (by the vigilante Azrael… and again later by Dick Grayson… and then again later still by Commissioner Gordon); being driven insane (by the twisted Doctor Hurt); even being killed (by Darkseid, malevolent godlike ruler of the planet Apokolips… although it transpired Batman was actually flung back in time). It has helped that, despite his propensity for working alone, he has surrounded himself by an extended "family" to aid him in his war on crime – various Robins; various Batgirls; Batwoman; Catwoman (on occasion); and others

besides – and he even founded a black ops-style team, the Outsiders, to hunt super-criminals.

Despite his dour countenance, Batman has proved he can be a team player. A founding member of the Justice League, while he has not always been comfortable around the superhuman powerhouses that largely comprise the group, he understands the global – even galactic – scale that the League operates on and the good that they can do. In particular, he has formed close bonds with Superman and Wonder Woman, beings possessed of power almost beyond imagination but whom Bruce calls friends.

Remarkably, for one more comfortable in the shadows, Batman has at times assumed leadership of the League, most memorably in 1987's *Justice League* series, written and drawn by Keith Giffen, J.M. DeMatteis, and Kevin Maguire. In that title, Batman shepherded a markedly misfit team that included Shazam, Blue Beetle, Mister Miracle, and stand-in Green Lantern Guy Gardner, a loudmouthed jerk of a hero who Batman, five issues into the series, was forced to knock unconscious (with one punch). More recently, Batman formed a Justice League of America to provide a more street level, human-scale sort of protection, recruiting a mixture of heroes and villains to the cause.

01
A panel from Batman's first comic appearance in 1939's *Detective Comics #27*

02
Batman's origin is covered in 1939's *Detective Comics #33*

03
The cover of Batman's first comic appearance – in *Detective Comics #27*

04
The dynamic duo – Batman & Robin from 1940's *Batman #1*

05
A shocking time for Batman as his second Robin (Jason Todd) is killed

06
A key moment of Bruce Wayne's life is recounted in 1987's critically acclaimed 'Batman: Year One' storyline

In general, however, Batman's role in the League has tended to be lower key – below the radar, as befits his status as an urban legend rather than a publicly visible hero. His standing as the team's master tactician became more pronounced from 1997 onwards, when writer Grant Morrison and artist Howard Porter launched *JLA*, a series which reunited the "big seven" heroes – Superman, Wonder Woman, Batman, Aquaman, The Flash (Wally West, the former Kid Flash), Green Lantern (Kyle Rayner), and Martian Manhunter. In this version of the League, it was just as likely that Batman would use his brains as his brawn to defeat an enemy – a state of affairs that persists to this day. ◾

GAL GADOT IS
WONDER WOMAN

Continuing the momentous success of her own groundbreaking box office hit, Gal Gadot returns in *Justice League* as Diana Prince – known to the world as Wonder Woman. Here she discusses what it means to play such an iconic character, and just how much fun she had on the *Justice League* set!

Justice League Collector's Edition: How would you describe your time working on Justice League?

Gal Gadot: It's been such an amazing experience. I shot *Justice League* straight after *Wonder Woman* – I didn't even realize that I had finished on *Wonder Woman*!

Working with so many talented people has been fantastic. My castmates have been amazing to work with. The cast is huge and there are so many different, unique personalities. It's been such a pleasure, and it's bittersweet that it must come to an end... until next time!

What was it like when you were in costumes on set with all the other actors?

Coming onto the *Justice League* set wearing my own costume felt like the most normal thing because I'd been doing it for six months [on *Wonder Woman*]. But wearing the costume and having everyone else wearing their own costumes was hilarious!

BIO

Gal Gadot was born in Petah Tikva, Israel. Gal started her career as a model and won the Miss Israel beauty pageant title in 2004. After two years of military service with the Israel Defense Force, where she worked as a combat trainer, Gal left to pursue her dream of acting. After appearing in the Israeli drama *Bubot*, Gadot landed the recurring role of Gisele Yashar in the *Fast and Furious* series of films, which in turn led her to securing the role of Wonder Woman in *Batman v Superman: Dawn of Justice*, and the hit film, *Wonder Woman*.

On the first three days we just kept on laughing because it felt so surreal. There are so many Super Heroes, and here we are finally standing and shooting the movie, all of us together. It was great.

Do you remember the core ideas of Wonder Woman that you first talked about with the filmmakers? How have those ideas carried through to this movie?

When I had the very first conversations about Wonder Woman, we had a very general conversation about the way they saw Wonder Woman and how I saw her, and where our ideas of the character actually met. We both had a very similar approach to who she is and the way she behaves.

She's different; she's the greatest warrior and she's a goddess, and she has such an amazing inner strength. But at the same time, she can be vulnerable and emotional, and she cares so much for people. She just wants to make the world a better place. She's not a warrior so much as she's a peace-seeker. But she'll fight if she needs to. ▶

Above left: Wonder Woman protecting innocents at the Court House   **Above right:** Wonder Woman makes a dramatic entrance!

01

"

DIANA CARES FOR PEOPLE IN THE SINCEREST WAY. SHE DOESN'T CARE FOR FAME, GLORY, OR THE CREDIT. SHE'S THERE TO HELP PEOPLE OUT.

"

▶ It's such a privilege to be able to play this character. She's so special. She's so unique and pure. I truly love this character.

What are your character's strengths?
This is such an opportunity to show the stronger side of women. The values that she fights for and everything that she stands for are so relevant for today's world. Fighting would be her last option. She would try to negotiate, she would try to see if she can figure things out in a different way. But when there are no other options, then she will go and use her power and fight.

What does it mean to play such an iconic hero?
I think that each and every one of us wants to be a hero. DC Comics heroes have so many real qualities, because they're not perfect. It makes us think that we can be heroes as well.

What do you see Diana's role being in the Justice League? What does she bring to the team?

Diana is so different from the other heroes. She's a great warrior, she's a goddess, and she's the glue that bonds them together as a team. She makes each and every one of them feel stronger and capable.

I think that one of Diana's most beautiful qualities is that she cares for people in the sincerest way. She doesn't care for fame, glory, or the credit. She's not there for that. She's there to help people out.

What attracted you to the role?
What attracted me so much to this character is that she is so many different things, and they combine in a beautiful way.

I think that everything Wonder Woman stands for is brilliant. She stands for justice and peace and wisdom and love and acceptance and compassion. All of these things are becoming rare in our world. And I think that if we can spread her messages and maybe inspire a few people, who knows what will happen? ⬛

03

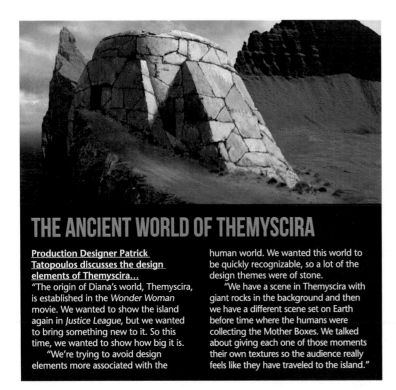

04

THE ANCIENT WORLD OF THEMYSCIRA

Production Designer Patrick Tatopoulos discusses the design elements of Themyscira...
"The origin of Diana's world, Themyscira, is established in the *Wonder Woman* movie. We wanted to show the island again in *Justice League*, but we wanted to bring something new to it. So this time, we wanted to show how big it is.

"We're trying to avoid design elements more associated with the human world. We wanted this world to be quickly recognizable, so a lot of the design themes were of stone.

"We have a scene in Themyscira with giant rocks in the background and then we have a different scene set on Earth before time where the humans were collecting the Mother Boxes. We talked about giving each one of those moments their own textures so the audience really feels like they have traveled to the island."

01
Diana Prince at
work in the Louvre

02
Diana in the
Bat Hangar

03
Wonder Woman
dives into action
(literally!)

04
A thoughtful moment
for Diana Prince

05
A rare moment
of calm for Wonder
Woman

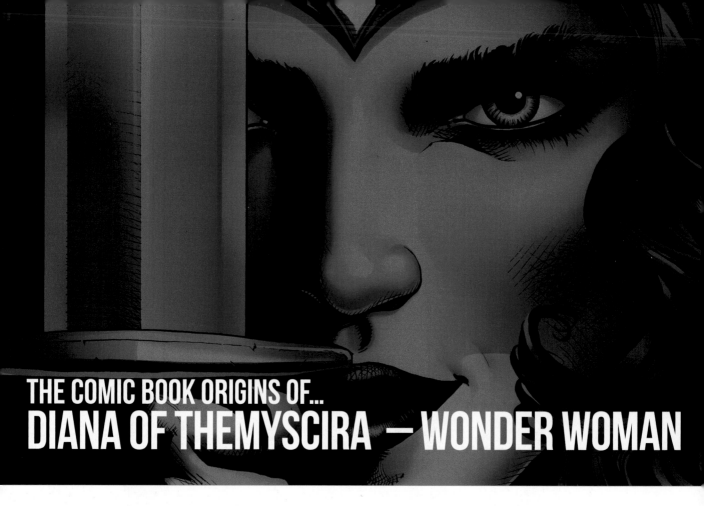

THE COMIC BOOK ORIGINS OF...
DIANA OF THEMYSCIRA — WONDER WOMAN

REAL NAME DIANA OF THEMYSCIRA/DIANA PRINCE

CREATED BY WILLIAM MOULTON MARSTON

FIRST APPEARANCE *ALL-STAR COMICS* #8 (OCTOBER 1941)

FIRST JOINED THE LEAGUE *BRAVE AND THE BOLD* (VOL. 1) #28 (MARCH 1960)

POWER AND ABILITIES A DEMI-GOD WITH A VARIETY OF POWERS – INCLUDING SUPERHUMAN STRENGTH, DURABILITY, SPEED, AND FLIGHT – WONDER WOMAN ALSO WIELDS A NUMBER OF WEAPONS, AMONG THEM HER UNBREAKABLE SILVER BRACELETS AND THE LASSO OF TRUTH.

Princess, ambassador, warrior: Wonder Woman has been all these and more. Her history is entwined with myth and legend, and her mission as emissary of the Amazons of Themyscira to Man's World has led her to join the Justice League, where she has formed unbreakable bonds with Superman, Batman and the rest of the team.

"As lovely as Aphrodite – as wise as Athena – with the speed of Mercury and the strength of Hercules – she is known only as Wonder Woman" – so ran the introduction in Wonder Woman's debut appearance in *All-Star Comics* #8. The ensuing story detailed how "the princess," as the narration referred to her, rescued Army Intelligence Captain

Steve Trevor from the wreckage of his plane after it crash-landed on Paradise Island, home to the Amazons, who long ago had settled there to escape the influence of men. Guided by the Goddesses Aphrodite and Athena, Hippolyte (later to become Hippolyta), the princess' mother, was determined to return Steve to America "to help fight the forces of hate and oppression," and wanted to send with him the "strongest and wisest Amazon." Accordingly, Hippolyte held a tournament to find the most capable of her subjects, but forbade her daughter from entering, for whoever went to America could never return. The princess entered anyway in disguise, and when she triumphed – thanks in part to her skilled wielding of her bullet-proof silver bracelets – Hippolyte named her Diana "after the Goddess of the Moon" and presented her with a costume.

The story continued in *Sensation Comics* #1 in January 1942, as Wonder Woman transported Steve back to Man's World in her "transparent plane," adopting the civilian identity of Diana Prince as a disguise and helping Steve foil a terrorist plot. *Sensation Comics* #2 saw Wonder Woman preventing the villainous "Doctor Poison" – who turned out to be an evil princess – from destroying the American Army; on that occasion, Diana was assisted by the loyal Etta

Candy, who would become her friend and sidekick. Meanwhile, the debut issue of Wonder Woman's own title that same year filled in some of the details of her origin, including her being molded from clay as a baby by her mother (under the direction of Athena), being presented with a "Magic Lasso," alias the Lasso of Truth, and rechristening her "transparent plane" as her Invisible Plane.

Over ensuing years, Wonder Woman and her world grew and developed. Shortly before she became a founding member of the Justice League in 1960, her comic book origins were revisited; *Wonder Woman* #98 (1958) depicted a revised account of the Amazonian contest and Steve's arrival on Paradise Island, while #105 recounted how the Amazons originally found Paradise Island. Later, in 1965's *Brave and the Bold* #60, Diana gained a sister, in the shape of Donna Troy, alias Wonder Girl. Later still, in 1968's *Wonder Woman* #179, Diana's status quo changed when the Amazons retreated to another dimension and she was deprived of her powers, having to rely instead on acquired martial arts skills.

In common with Superman and others of DC Comics' heroes, in the wake of the 1985 reality-reordering event *Crisis on Infinite Earths* – at the climax of which Diana was killed by the evil Anti-Monitor – Wonder Woman was

reinvigorated for a modern audience. In the hands of artist/writer team George Perez and Greg Potter, Diana's origin was retold to emphasize her link with the Olympian Gods, with Paradise Island now identified as Themyscira. Guided by Athena, Hermes, and other Gods, Diana was dispatched to Man's World on a mission to locate and defeat Ares, the God of War.

It was the springboard for a bold new era for Wonder Woman, as the previously hidden Amazons announced themselves to the world, and a war erupted between the Olympian and Roman Gods. Not long after, Diana lost her powers and

was replaced as Wonder Woman for a time by her Amazonian rival Artemis – although Diana, who at that time was leader of the Justice League, retained that leadership role after her teammates rallied round her. Toward the end of the 1990s, Diana was again temporarily replaced as Wonder Woman, this time by her own mother, Hippolyta.

As the 2000s unfolded, Wonder Woman's role of Amazonian ambassador to Man's World took on a more concrete aspect, as she opened a Themysciran Embassy in New York. Since then, Wonder Woman has undergone a number of seismic changes – notably

06
Variant cover artwork by Stanley Lau from the first Wonder Woman: Rebirth issue

following the 2011 "New 52" relaunch, when she was reimagined as a demi-goddess (with Zeus as her father and Hippolyta as her mother) – and has recently returned to her roots as Amazonian emissary of peace and justice in Man's World as part of DC's "Rebirth" relaunch. ▪

JASON MOMOA IS
AQUAMAN

From *Conan the Barbarian* to *Game of Thrones'* Khal Drogo, Aquaman is the latest fantasy warrior to be brought to life by actor Jason Momoa. Now shooting the *Aquaman* movie, the Hawaiian-born star reveals what it was like bringing Arthur Curry and Aquaman to the Justice League...

Justice League Collector's Edition: Who is Aquaman?

Jason Momoa: Aquaman is Arthur Curry... But I don't think Arthur Curry believes he is Aquaman yet. Curry is hiding on the edges of society, hanging out with the riff-raff and the dredges. He's in a place where they respect him because he can bring in food and help people. He's a lone wolf.

Would you say he's caught between two worlds?

What I love about Arthur/Aquaman in *Justice League* is that he hasn't accepted himself as a king. He's been running from both sides. To me he's like Josey Wales from the Clint Eastwood movie, *The Outlaw Josey Wales*. He's so defiant, and then he meets the Justice League and they become this family.

Do you identify with Arthur at all?

I can identify with Arthur. I was born in Hawaii and then raised in Iowa where it's all cornfields, so it's something I can relate to. Arthur doesn't really know where he fits in in our world and I was different too, but it was fine.

BIO

Jason Momoa was born in Honolulu, Hawaii. After leaving university with a degree in Marine Biology, Momoa started his acting career in television, securing recurring roles in several TV shows including *Baywatch Hawaii* as Jason Loane and in *North Shore* as Frankie Seau. It was his role as Ronon Dex in the TV show *Stargate Atlantis*, which ran from 2004 to 2009, that finally established him as an actor of note. In 2011, he was cast as Robert E. Howard's Conan the Barbarian and then as the barbarian warrior Khal Drogo in the award-winning HBO series *Game of Thrones*. His presence and performances landed him the role of Aquaman, first appearing in *Batman v Superman: Dawn of Justice*.

Then I go home to Hawaii – on the very Hawaiian side – I'm not really accepted. I was the haole *(a local term referring to people not descended from native Hawaiians – Ed.)*, so I just thought, "Okay, I'll find my own path in this world."

Is Aquaman's attitude one reason why he's so reluctant to join Bruce Wayne's cause?

They see his talents and they need his talents to help the world, but he's not really great at working with others – and that's what gives you the drama and comedy. Finally, when he knows that the world is in danger, he gets it together. We become the closest we can be as a family, and then we break off into our own worlds again, but we still come together as an army and help one another. That's what's great about the Justice League.

This journey started for you on *Batman v Superman*, and will continue in *Aquaman*. How do you feel about the character at this point?

He knows what his power is, but he doesn't know how to channel it, so this movie is like a coming of age for my character.

I was excited to know more about Aquaman, because we hadn't learned much about him in *Batman v Superman*. Now it's solidified, and it's a great feeling to know that these last seven months I've really been able to put in the time, finding pieces of myself to put into this character.

He's not supposed to be the king of Atlantis yet, but he has these powers, and this defiance to become something that he was ▶

Jason Momoa as Arthur Curry / Aquaman

▶ destined to be. We're just starting on this gigantic arc that's going to continue on for – who knows? – another 10 years.

How much preparation did you do for the role of Aquaman?
I trained really hard for *Batman v Superman* just for one day of work, and I'd never done a Super Hero film before. That was really terrifying, because you come onto a set that's been shooting for months, and everyone knows each other, then you come in for one day. Everyone is kind of quiet, and they look at you, and you come on and shoot one underwater scene against a green screen and then you're wrapped. And you've trained so hard to get your body into that shape!

Let's talk about your costumes. Arthur has a very lived-in look, but Aquaman has something iconic about him.
It's amazing. Everyone's armor is unbelievable, but mine is beautiful. It's gold and green, and weighs about 40 pounds. I don't know what it's made out of, but it's heavy. You put it on, and you sink right into the character.

For Arthur, [Costume Designer] Michael Wilkinson really embraced how I dress in daily life, which was cool. You have to rule out a lot of normal clothes, so we were like, "You've got to go for a rock 'n' roll hobo/dirty vagabond kind of thing." And I said, "I've got some things in

01

02

03

my wardrobe we could use – I've got some dirty clothes."

My character's look is kind of a mix of rock 'n' roll and tribal stuff. I live out of a bag most of the time, and I like to wear little things that remind me of home. Arthur has lots of collectibles and trinkets and rings and necklaces – odd things here and there – because Arthur lives on the road and he's constantly moving. It's so great when you work with creative artists who embrace your ideas. That's how Arthur was born, between Michael Wilkinson and me.

What do you think about the other characters' costumes?
I freaked out when I saw Batman. I was like a geek, a total kid!

And then you see the unglamorous side of it… You're sweating and it's hot and it sucks – you've been in your costume for 12 hours. I've got these contact lenses, and they can be pretty intense if you're in the smoke and dirt – but you're all in pain together so it's pretty funny.

Give me some thoughts on your castmates. Let's start with Gal Gadot.
Amazing, beautiful. I love working with her – it's like reaching into someone's soul and listening. Not acting, just listening to each other. Gal's the perfect Wonder Woman.

And Henry Cavill?
I love Henry. He's really given me a lot of tips on how to handle this whole thing, because he's been in it longer than the rest of us. He's been in the costumes, he knows the work schedule, the training. He's just dedicated.

> ## AQUAMAN IS JUST STARTING ON THIS GIGANTIC ARC THAT'S GOING TO CONTINUE ON FOR [POSSIBLY] ANOTHER 10 YEARS…

What about Ben Affleck?
I love goofing around with him. He really is just like a big brother. I'm super-stoked to know that we'll be together for a long time doing this. I really would love to work for him someday – to be in one of his movies. He's an amazing director. He's one of our executive producers too, so if I have any concerns, it's really cool to go to him as an actor and he knows every side of this business. It's reassuring.

Ezra Miller?
I've known Ezra since he was probably 15 or 16. He's a mad, crazy little genius, an uber artist. He brings in a big ball of life and makes me giggle.

Finally, Ray Fisher?
Ray's a badass. Super-dedicated. To me he is the thespian of the group. He loves the craft, and he works out super hard. He has the hardest job out of everyone in the sense that I put everything on, I put the contact lenses in, and I look like a badass – but he's in polka-dot pajamas, since his suit is CG, and he's not scary at all! It's just Ray in pajamas. Cyborg-life is pretty intense, so I'm super proud of him.

When I look at everyone in our cast, and this is 100 percent truthful, I think everyone is great. Ezra is perfect for Barry Allen. Ray Fisher is perfect for Cyborg. Wonder Woman, perfect. Henry's the best Superman. Batman, that's him, Ben Affleck. And no one, I mean no one, could play Aquaman better than me!

You've spent a lot of time talking to the cinematographer, Fabian Wagner, during the shoot, and you're a big fan of cameras and photography. Is that a direction you see yourself heading toward in the future?
I figure I'm getting paid to go to school. At the end of the day, I want to be a storyteller, but I've got a distinctive look that means I'm not going to fit certain roles. So if there are stories that I'm not going to be a part of, I want to be behind the camera. I want to help a director see his vision through.

I love cinematography because the truth of it is, as an actor, I would like to strip away all dialogue, to see if I can tell a story through composition, through body movement, through lighting. I mean, I can make my performance better just by lighting it right and seeing that it's captured with the right lens.

What's next for you when this movie wraps?
I'll take a little break for about a month, and eat pasta, get fat for a while, and then get back into shape for *Aquaman*. I'm excited to see where we're going with it all. 🖤

01
Jason Momoa as Aquaman

02
Jason Momoa being filmed on location in Iceland

03
Jason on set with Zack Snyder

04
Aquaman and Wonder Woman prepare for battle

05
Jason Momoa in his full Aquaman outfit

THE COMIC BOOK ORIGINS OF...
ARTHUR CURRY — AQUAMAN

REAL NAME
ARTHUR CURRY

CREATED BY MORT
WEISINGER AND PAUL
NORRIS

FIRST APPEARANCE
MORE FUN COMICS
#73 (NOVEMBER 1941)

**FIRST JOINED THE
LEAGUE** *BRAVE AND
THE BOLD* (VOL. 1) #28
(MARCH 1960)

POWER AND ABILITIES
POSSESSED OF
GREAT STRENGTH
AND DURABILITY
AND THE ABILITY TO
BREATHE UNDERWATER,
AQUAMAN CAN ALSO
COMMUNICATE WITH
AND COMMAND
AQUATIC LIFE VIA
TELEPATHY.

Ruler of Atlantis, King of the Seven Seas, Aquaman is a hero of two worlds – the world beneath the waves, and the world above. With the vast expanse of the Earth's oceans to oversee, it would be reasonable to assume that the surface world might be a secondary concern, yet Aquaman has always been there when most needed by the Justice League, lending his strength, courage, and regal authority.

Though Aquaman was given an origin of sorts in his comics debut in 1940 (in the same issue of *More Fun* in which fellow Justice Leaguer Green Arrow also debuted) – claiming he was able to live underwater thanks to his undersea explorer father, who had trained him using the records and devices of the lost Kingdom of Atlantis – it was significantly revised in 1959. In *Adventure Comics* #260, Aquaman revealed that he is Arthur Curry, the son of a human lighthouse-keeper, Tom Curry, and an exiled denizen of Atlantis, Atlanna. Inheriting his mother's abilities to live underwater and communicate with sea creatures, Arthur developed powerful telepathy, allowing him to control and command aquatic life. Having divulged all of this to a naval commander in an effort to halt an underwater nuclear weapons test, Aquaman dove beneath the waves to gaze upon his ancestral home, a huge civilization called Atlantis that he one day hoped to return to.

Gradually, a mythology accumulated around Aquaman, built upon by successive writers and artists. He gained a junior partner, Aqualad, alias Atlantean reject Garth; a love interest, Mera; a half-brother (on his father's side), Orm, who became his nemesis Ocean Master; and a kingdom, the aforementioned Atlantis, which he became monarch of in the 18th issue of his own series in 1964. Making Mera his queen in that same issue, Aquaman would before long gain a son, too.

Aquaman and Mera's underwater wedding was attended by his Justice League teammates Superman, Wonder Woman, Martian Manhunter, The Flash, The Atom, and Batman (with Robin) – Aquaman having joined the League at its foundation. Some time later, Aquaman himself led an incarnation of the League. In 1984's *Justice League of America Annual* #2, following the destruction of the Justice League satellite, Aquaman returned to Atlantis, only to be confronted by a recording of Mera informing him that, distraught over the recent death of their son – killed by Black Manta – she had decided to leave Arthur. Crushed, Aquaman headed to the United Nations to announce that, with the League's most powerful members – Superman, Wonder Woman, The Flash, and Green Lantern – all at that time absent from the roster, he was disbanding the League and replacing it with a new version, one composed of full-time, committed members. Accordingly, with the help of new member Steel and joined by fellow street-level newbie Leaguers Vibe and Gypsy, Aquaman's Justice League established a new headquarters in Detroit – an urban fortress housed in an old factory.

Aquaman's own involvement with that team was rather short-lived, curtailed the following year when he was reunited with Mera and quit the League hoping to rediscover his life. But instead of heralding a period of calm for Arthur, it was the beginning of a time of tumultuous

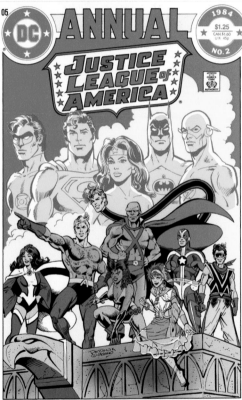

change. Initially this change was merely cosmetic – Aquaman gained a new blue costume in 1986 – but as the years wore on, the changes became more stark. In the 1989 *Legend of Aquaman* one-shot, Arthur's origin was revised so that he was now a full Atlantean – albeit one with pale skin and blond hair – who had been rejected from the city of Poseidonis as a baby and raised by lighthouse keeper Arthur Curry, from whom he gained his name. That origin – and the history of Atlantis itself – was significantly expanded upon by writer Peter David's 1990 and 1993 mini-series *Atlantis Chronicles* (with artist Esteban Maroto) and *Aquaman: Time and Tide* (with artist Kirk Jarvinen), before David took Aquaman in an even more radical direction by bestowing upon him a beard, having his right hand eaten away by piranha, and then replacing that hand with a harpoon.

Since then, Aquaman has been transformed into living water; mutated into a malformed being called the Dweller in the Depths (and been replaced by a younger Aquaman); died and been resurrected; and finally returned to his original status quo as half-human defender of the oceans.

As part of DC's "New 52" relaunch, for a time Aquaman walked (or even swam) away from his Atlantean throne, basing himself in Boston, where, with Mera by his side, he protected the surface-dwellers from the Trench, savage invaders hailing from the Marianas Trench. But when an Ocean Master-led Atlantis declared war on the surface world, Aquaman and his allies in the Justice League raced to the defense of humanity, after which Arthur reclaimed his throne from Orm. 🗡

EZRA MILLER IS
THE FLASH

Award-winning actor Ezra Miller takes up the mantle
of Barry Allen, a.k.a. The Flash, as the speedy Super Hero
makes his big-screen debut in *Justice League*. Here he reveals
his thoughts on The Flash's costume, his castmates, and
what he would like to steal from the set...!

**Justice League Collector's Edition:
It's your last day on set. How does
that feel?**
Ezra Miller: It's the end of an
era and the birth of a hero. I feel
melancholic, but it's beautiful,
man. I'm so thankful. It's bittersweet, but it's amazing.

**How has it been, working on such
a big movie?**
I feel proud that we've done this.
I've been here for eight months,
well over half a year of my life.
We've been here at Leavesden Studios,
working so hard. We're talking six-day
weeks, 10 to 13-hour days. There are
800 people on this crew and we've
all been coming together and
working our tails off, making
very serious commitments and
contributions. We've really gone
hard and I feel proud of everybody –
including myself!

We found a really beautiful
family here. It's just a beautiful
thing, because it feels like we've
all supported each other through
it. And that's what this movie is
ultimately about, in the stripped-
down sense.

BIO
Actor, singer,
and musician **Ezra
Miller** was born in
Wyckoff, New Jersey.
He started his acting
career at the age of 16
in the film *Afterschool*.
In 2011, he took the
lead role in the critically
acclaimed *We Need to
Talk About Kevin* and
in 2015 he co-starred
in both *The Stanford
Prison Experiment*
and the comedy-
drama *Trainwreck*.
In 2016, he appeared
in *Fantastic Beasts
and Where to Find
Them* and had in
a cameo role as
The Flash in *Batman
v Superman: Dawn
of Justice* .

**What's it like working with the
producers on set?**
Zack Snyder is the DC god. He's the
father of our universe. He's been
directing this series of films that
will really plant the seeds for the
whole Gaia tree of the DC Universe,
and its many branches and flowers,
giving us, the cast, this template
as an artistic community. Zack has
really taken care of us all. He's been
so incredibly attentive to all of us
and our diva needs and our questions.
And when I want to overthink the
physics of The Flash, he's been ready
to engage with me on that level.

So what are the physics of The Flash?
Okay, so there's a way that you could
perceive The Flash, which is that
he's fast, right? Boring! Or, you can
perceive him as I do, as what I might
refer to as a quantum vibrator. He
brings to the Justice League this extra-
dimensional power, wherein he plays
within the reality of time and space,
which of course, as we know from
recent physical evidence that supports
Einstein's theory of relativity, time
and space are one entity. And this
entity not only bends, but it jiggles. ▶

Above left: The Flash powers up **Above right:** The Flash catches a Batarang with his speed powers

01

▶ **That sounds like quite an acting challenge...**

I feel a deep sense of gratitude to have had such a strange and delightful task. I entered this movie really thinking a lot about the forces to call on, in terms of the physical vocabulary that this character lives in. There were people who have been major aides to my process on other films, who I thought about reaching out to, to work out that movement/linguistic invention, and then I decided to do this on my own. It's been massively affirming for me to do that, to feel even in the most minor sense that I've accomplished the task.

You're a comic book fan. What was it like when you had everybody on set together, in costume?

So a-maz-ing! It's very hard to describe the feeling when you look out and you see an Alex Ross painting, right in front of you, and it's these real people. And there's this underlying knowledge of everything these characters have done, and gone through, to get to that place. I swear, I've been blacking out and

entering comic frames, then coming round in this invented universe and thinking, "Where am I?!"

And how did you feel about your own costume?

Unbelievably fantastic. It's amazing. I feel coddled. I could take a nap really easily in this thing, because it's like a nice, silky blanket, just wrapped up real tight. It's a bit like mummification, but I still have my brains and internal organs. I'll always know what it feels like to be a sausage, in intestinal casing. So if I ever were to get a script where someone's a sausage… or someone

> ## "
> ## THE FLASH COSTUME IS AMAZING. I COULD TAKE A NAP REALLY EASILY IN THIS THING, BECAUSE IT'S LIKE A NICE, SILKY BLANKET, JUST WRAPPED UP REAL TIGHT. I'LL ALWAYS KNOW WHAT IT FEELS LIKE TO BE A SAUSAGE.
> ## "

becomes a sausage… I'll take it, because I know the depths of that role!

Do you feel as if the cast has formed a league, as much as the characters?

I've been saying, I'm actually feeling at this point in my life, that if I were to have to squad-up and enter some sort of physical conflict, the crew of friends I would choose to have with me in a bar fight would be my fellow *Justice League* cast members. I couldn't think of anyone who's more ready to stand by each other's side and fight for each other, because we've done it. You fight through the 13-hour workday.

We don't use lassos of truth, we use candies of sugar, coffees of caffeine, and friendship, and fun, and humor. And not just the cast, but this entire crew, this amazing group of creative people who have been supporting each other as we slog through this.

So, are you ready to go through it all again for *The Flash* movie?

I'm ready to go right now. Honestly, I'm just getting warmed up. I'm ready to go. I am criminally excited to be a part of the *Justice League*. I'm having too much fun. There should be rules.

What props would you like to take away with you from this shoot?

What am I taking away with me? I'm going to steal the watch, Barry's watch. I'd like to take a suit home if I can, so that I can run up to people in the night and freak them out. And I'm stealing some costumes, and maybe a prop or two. I'd like an Atlantean sword, or an Amazonian shield. I might try to steal one of Batman's harpoon guns or something. ∎

'FL-YBORG'

Producer Deborah Snyder discusses Ezra Miller and Ray Fisher's rapport on set…
"A nice thing has happened between Ray as Cyborg and Ezra as Flash, because they're the youngest members of the Justice League. There's a real connection when they interact – it's almost like they're buddies. It's nice to see that dynamic as a fan, and it's great to see what their performances are growing into."

THE COMIC BOOK ORIGINS OF...
BARRY ALLEN – THE FLASH

REAL NAME
BARRY ALLEN

CREATED BY ROBERT
KANIGHER AND
CARMINE INFANTINO

FIRST APPEARANCE
SHOWCASE #4
(OCTOBER 1956)

**FIRST JOINED THE
LEAGUE** *BRAVE AND
THE BOLD* (VOL. 1) #28
(MARCH 1960)

POWER AND ABILITIES
ABLE TO RUN AT
INCREDIBLE VELOCITIES,
BARRY ALLEN CAN ALSO
USE HIS SUPER-SPEED
TO VIBRATE HIS BODY,
GENERATE CYCLONES,
AND HEAL HIMSELF
RAPIDLY WHEN INJURED.

As The Flash – the Fastest Man Alive – Barry Allen has played a pivotal role in the history of the Justice League, speeding into action at times of great crisis, prepared to make the ultimate sacrifice. But just as important in the story of the Scarlet Speedster is the notion of legacy – of the mantle of The Flash being passed from hero to hero.

Unlike Superman, Batman, and many other of the original Justice League members, Barry Allen wasn't the first super-speedster to be called The Flash. That honor was held by Jay Garrick, the "Golden Age" Flash, a tin-hatted hero who raced into action in 1940 in *Flash Comics* #1. A charter member of the Justice League's super-team predecessors the Justice Society of America, Jay Garrick had faded from view by the early 1950s, like most of his teammates.

In 1956, The Flash was reimagined as Barry Allen, a police scientist granted the gift of super-speed when a bolt of lightning struck a cabinet in his lab and smashed the containers therein, bathing him in chemicals. Inspired by the original Flash – who, in Barry's world, was merely a character in a comic book (!) – Barry decided to "use this unique speed to help humanity!" He created a red costume –

which, unlike his comic book forebear, incorporated a mask (in a back-up story in *Flash* #128, it would be revealed that Barry had settled on being masked after having a daydream where public acclaim had hampered his Flash activities), and which he kept compressed inside a ring on his finger – and embarked on a crime-fighting career as the all-new Flash.

He was the first of a wave of revitalized versions of Golden Age characters – a "Silver Age" that would soon see new versions of Green Lantern, The Atom, and Hawkman, all of whom would join Barry in the Justice League. Meanwhile, launched into his own title in 1959 (which inherited the numbering of the original *Flash* comic, #105), The Flash faced a succession of bizarre villains, including Captain Cold, the Mirror Master, the Pied Piper, the Weather Wizard, the Trickster, Captain Boomerang, Heat Wave and The Top – who would team up in various combinations over ensuing years, coming to be known collectively as the Rogues. There was also the persistent nemesis Professor Zoom, alias the Reverse-Flash.

Not content with kicking off the Silver Age, Barry Allen was also instrumental in the birth of the multiverse – the concept that there were many parallel realities in the DC Universe, not just one. In the story "Flash of Two Worlds" in *Flash* #123 (1961),

01

02

03

Barry used his super-speed to vibrate so fast that he accidentally tore a gap in reality and wound up on a parallel Earth – one where an older Jay Garrick was real, but had retired as The Flash. After reasoning that original *Flash* writer Gardner Fox must have somehow "tuned into" Jay's Earth when asleep and "dreamed up" the first Flash's adventures in comic book form, Barry and Jay teamed up to solve a series of mysterious robberies. It was the first of many team-ups not only for the two Flashes, but between the Justice League and Justice Society.

The concept of the DC multiverse would prove instrumental in Barry Allen's downfall. In the epic 1985 mini-series *Crisis on Infinite Earths*, after two and a half decades of adventures in his own title and in *Justice League of America*, Barry was killed preventing the reality-destroying Anti-Monitor from bringing about the end of everything. Thereafter, the mantle of The Flash passed to Wally West – Barry's nephew and former junior sidekick Kid Flash (who, remarkably, had gained super-speed in a repeat of the accident that had given Barry his powers). Like Barry, Wally became a mainstay of the Justice League and

01
Barry Allen makes his first appearance as The Flash in *Showcase* Vol. 1 #4, from 1956

02
Things start to get complicated in *The Flash* #123 from 1961

03
Tragedy strikes in 1985's *Crisis on Infinite Earths* #8

04
The shocking death of Barry Allen from *Crisis on Infinite Earths* #8

05
Things get even more complicated in 2011's *Flashpoint* mini-series

06
The original Flash from 1940

07
Splash page from *Showcase* Vol. 1 #4

battled his own Rogues, until he too passed on the mantle of The Flash, this time to Bart Allen, alias Impulse, grandson of Barry and his wife Iris from the far future (where Barry and Iris retired for a time), a young hero who was himself killed not long after (although he later returned to life).

But Barry's story was by no means done. After abortive resurrections in the 1993 storyline "The Return of Barry Allen" ("Barry" turned out to be Professor Zoom) and the 2005 miniseries *Infinite Crisis*, he was finally brought back into being in the midst of another

crisis – 2008's *Final Crisis* (the same mini-series which saw the apparent demise of Batman). After a subsequent miniseries, *Flash: Rebirth*, revealed that Barry originally became a police scientist to try and prove his father innocent of the murder of his mother, he resumed his place at the heart of the Justice League. Aptly, given his central role in previous crises, he was instrumental in a wholesale remaking of the DC Universe in the 2011 event *Flashpoint*, which launched DC's "New 52" initiative, and which identified Barry's mother's murderer as a time-traveling Professor Zoom. ◗

RAY FISHER IS
CYBORG

Created by writer Marv Wolfman and artist George Pérez for DC Comics in 1980, Cyborg joined the DC Extended Universe with a cameo appearance in Zack Snyder's 2016 movie, *Batman v Superman: Dawn of Justice*. The man/machine is back in *Justice League*, and filling the Cyborg role once more is actor Ray Fisher...

Justice League Collector's Edition: What does it feel like to become part of the DC Universe? Were you a Super Hero fan when you were growing up?
Ray Fisher: It feels like the wheel has come full circle. I grew up watching *Batman* and I watched *Batman Returns* every Christmas. I'd tie a towel around my shoulders and would jump off my porch pretending I was Superman. And now here I am, involved in all this! I couldn't have dreamed for it to unfold the way it did, and I can't imagine a better experience. As far as I'm concerned, if this is the only thing I'm blessed to do, then I'm glad it was for something that meant so much to me as a kid. Hopefully it'll mean a lot to other kids out there.

What can you tell us about Victor Stone, a.k.a. Cyborg?
Victor is half-man, half-machine, and *all* hero. In our version he's a college athlete, a quarterback, and he's a genius with an IQ of 170. In order to save Victor's life after an accident, his father uses a Mother

BIO

Ray Fisher was born in Camden, New Jersey. After attending the American Musical and Dramatic Academy in New York, Ray embarked on a career in theater, performing with the Shakespeare Theatre of New Jersey in a production of *Macbeth* and also in *To Kill a Mockingbird*. It was his role as Muhammad Ali in the 2013 off-Broadway production of *Fetch Clay, Make Man* (for which he gained 20 pounds) that led to him being cast as Cyborg in the new DC movies.

Box to implant cybernetic technology into his body, and those cybernetics give him new abilities that he's discovering every day like super strength and the ability to fly. He's patched into every computer on the face of the planet, and he's a "technopath," so he can interface with anything technological.

But half his face is completely cybernetic, and that's one of his big issues. He has to overcome the physical appearance of being half-man/half-machine, and it ends up preventing him from living what we would consider to be a normal life. That's a big part of his journey, trying to find that normalcy that comes along with who he now is.

Another part of Victor's journey is dealing with the alien portion of his body and not being fully in control of it. He discovers there are moments where he's not quite sure how his cybernetic defenses will react to certain stressful situations and dealing with this unknown duality inside of himself. He has to trust that even though he's now part Apokoliptian technology, that ▶

Above: Ray Fisher has to adjust to becoming a half-man/half-machine Super Hero in *Justice League*

▶ Victor's human element is still in charge and fighting for justice.

How do you prepare yourself for a role like this?

There are a lot of different levels to play, so I was really excited to be able to dig in and explore Cyborg. The big thing about Victor Stone is he's trying to rediscover his place in this world. We get into the interactions between Victor and Silas Stone, his father, and that's where a lot of the emotional heart of the character is. I think Cyborg is the perfect combination of the power of technology and the strength of the human heart.

As Cyborg deals with his own issues, how does that affect his relationship with the rest of the Justice League?

There's a very interesting team dynamic in how Cyborg and the other characters interact with one another. You have five different people from five very different backgrounds, and they're all trying to figure each other out *and* what they're supposed to do in their own worlds. So, there are a lot of different layers, and a lot of different things to play with.

Cyborg's human muscles are all you. Did you realize that there would be so much training when you got the role?

I played Muhammad Ali in a piece

01
Members of the League prepare for battle

02
Ray Fisher as football star Victor Stone

03
Cyborg prepares for battle in the Knightcrawler

04
Cyborg leads the way with the Justice League

CGI CYBORG

JL Collector's Edition: Cyborg will be realized primarily through CGI, but your performance is being translated through motion capture. Can you explain how that works?
Ray Fisher: "I wear a performance capture suit, covered in all these dots, which are there to capture the mobility and motion of Cyborg. I've got this chest light, so you can see the core of Cyborg glowing, and we've got a ping pong ball with LED lights in it, to give us a little bit of an idea as to the kind of light that Cyborg's eye will be casting out. That way we can have the light he emits fall in appropriate places on other people, as well as myself."

> # THE BIG THING ABOUT VICTOR STONE IS HE'S TRYING TO REDISCOVER HIS PLACE IN THIS WORLD. THE INTERACTIONS BETWEEN VICTOR AND SILAS STONE ARE WHERE THE EMOTIONAL HEART OF THE CHARACTER IS.

that involved a bit of training, but that was training that I was doing primarily on my own. I had a boxing consultant on that, who was helping me get in shape. I knew that there would be some working out for this movie – that's just a part of the process – but I didn't know it was going to be as rigorous as it's been. Trying to build up this quarterback physique is grueling, but it's good. Twenty pounds in, I feel like my body's just started to adjust to being a bit heavier. This is the heaviest I think I've ever been, and it takes some getting used to, but it feels like it's as natural a part of me as anything else now. It's definitely the most difficult thing I've ever done in my life. I'm just a guy from New Jersey with asthma, coming in and training five days a week, two hours a day, all the food, all the calories... But I'm not complaining about that, you know – give an actor a free meal!

Did being asthmatic make you feel uneasy about taking on such a physical role?

I haven't had very many issues recently with it. It's exercise-induced, but the way that I got over it was by trying to work through it and trying to build up lung capacity. We've got good guys in here to keep us motivated and keep us in it. Mark Twight and Stu Walton are training me and making sure I get to the size I need in a healthy and safe way. I've eaten more food than I've ever eaten in my life, lifted more weights than I've ever lifted in my life. I've sweated and cried more than I've ever sweated and cried in my life. Mark and Stu have been absolutely influential in getting all this stuff together. It's easier when you just come out of the gym. You're all pumped up and ready to go. It's one of those things where you can

actually see the fruits of your labor and you know something's working.

How have you enjoyed bringing the Cyborg character to life?

It's been an absolute blast. And there's probably not a bigger fan on the planet, myself included, that knows as much about these comics as Zack Snyder does. Zack is, first and foremost, a storyteller. He has a very specific visual style, and he gets recognized for that, but he delves deeply into these characters too. For an actor, it's thrilling to be a part of, because you have somebody that understands where these characters are coming from.

Can you describe how you and the filmmakers worked together to figure out the Cyborg character?

It's one of the most collaborative efforts I think I've ever had. Zack really listens, he really takes in what it is that you have to say, and he really respects your opinions. At the end of the day, everybody wants the same thing for the story, which is the best possible story that we can put out there.

Zack and I spent hours and hours chatting about Cyborg, mapping out his journey, refining and revisiting these things time and time again, because as things shift and change, and as we find things on the day, it might affect something that's happening to him later on down the line. We kept in constant contact about this guy's journey, his emotional connection to his father, how Victor has to deal with this thing that is now a part of his life for a very different reason. I think the way the crew shoot a lot of these things – the style and the tone – really caters to that journey and to that emotional arc.

This is a huge film, with some enormous sets. Was that intimidating at all?

It can be nerve-wracking, but my job is still the same. I'm an actor. I go on set, I do the scene to the best of my ability, and that's my job. And everybody on set has got a specific job to do. We've got thousands of people who are doing thousands of different jobs to make this whole thing come together. As long as I show up on time, know my lines and know what I'm doing, I'll be fine.

We have people working on this who have been fans since they

were kids, and it's all been like one big family unit. It's beautiful to see that exist in such a large-scale production. It makes it feel like home, and that beats anything else that you could be a part of.

Was the day when the entire Justice League suited up for the first time a special moment?

I'm in my CGI pajamas and everybody else is in their real Super Hero suits (*laughs*). It was like watching my eight-year-old dreams come true. It took me back to those days growing up, watching the cartoons. I caught myself humming the theme to the *Justice League* animated series while we were shooting that scene. The camera is spinning around, and we're all humming the theme song. It was really special.

Being able to watch the playback and see how that final shot of the film is going to look, it was beautiful. You finally see them all there, and it's the Justice League. I almost shed a tear, I will say. I held it together pretty good.

You're going to be known as Cyborg for quite a while. How do you feel about that?

Good! I feel good. That's what Cyborg life is all about, man. It's about taking the negative situations in your life and turning them into something positive for the people. So, if I become in any way synonymous with that, I'm fine with it. ◗

THE COMIC BOOK ORIGINS OF...
VICTOR STONE — CYBORG

REAL NAME
VICTOR STONE

CREATED BY
MARV WOLFMAN AND
GEORGE PEREZ

FIRST APPEARANCE *DC
COMICS PRESENTS* #26
(OCTOBER 1980)

**FIRST JOINED THE
LEAGUE** *JUSTICE LEAGUE
OF AMERICA* (VOL. 2) #41
(MARCH 2010); REVISED:
JUSTICE LEAGUE (VOL. 2)
#6 (APRIL 2012)

POWER AND ABILITIES
CYBERNETIC IMPLANTS
GRANT ENHANCED
STRENGTH, SPEED,
AND DURABILITY, ALONG
WITH ARM CANNONS,
INFRARED VISION, AND
BOOT JETS; ABLE TO
OPEN TELEPORTATION
BOOM TUBES.

He is a walking technological miracle – part man, part machine, all hero. His body a mash-up of super-advanced technology and all-too-human flesh, Cyborg is both a founding member of the Justice League and a relative newbie – depending on which era of comics you are reading…

Cyborg originally made his comics debut in 1980 as a member of the New Teen Titans, a revamped, reinvigorated take on the classic sidekick super-team. A high school sports star who had turned to football, athletics, and boxing after rejecting the more brainy pursuits his scientist parents had mapped out

for him, Victor Stone's life changed after an experiment in his mom and dad's lab went awry. An extra-dimensional portal that his father, Silas, had opened unleashed a monstrous creature – one that partially consumed Vic. To save his son's life, Silas replaced the lost body parts with powerful cybernetic ones – molybdenum steel for bone, plastics and polymers for flesh.

Vic's new physique granted him incredible strength, speed, and durability, as well as an array of sonic weaponry, infrared vision, and the ability to interface with computers. No longer able to fit in at school, Vic decided to put his new abilities to noble use, stopping an old

friend from blowing up the UN Building. Not long after, he joined Robin, Wonder Girl, Changeling (formerly Beast Boy), Kid Flash, and Raven in the newly reformed Teen Titans. Calling himself Cyborg, he helped his new friends prevent another (!) attack on the UN – this time by extraterrestrial slavers the Gordanians (an episode which saw alien princess Starfire join the group). Following this, Cyborg became a mainstay of the team.

Over time, Cyborg went through many changes, his cybernetic body upgraded, destroyed, and recreated on multiple occasions. For a while he became linked to the alien hive-mind Technis, an experience that saw him losing much of his humanity. Then known as Cyberion, he transformed the Moon into a Technis construct, bringing him into conflict with both his former Titans teammates and the Justice League (in 1998, in the three-issue *JLA/Titans* miniseries). Thanks to the efforts of the two super-teams, Cyborg regained his lost humanity, thereafter mentoring the next generation of young heroes in a new version of the Teen Titans.

For much of his Super Hero career Cyborg has been primarily associated with various incarnations of the Titans, but latterly he has become linked to the Justice League. He came close to joining the World's Greatest Super Heroes in

01

02

03

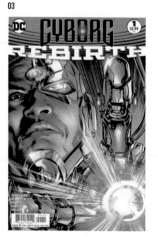

2006 (in *Justice League of America* Vol. 2 #3), but it wasn't until his Teen Titans teammates Donna Troy (the former Wonder Girl), Batman (at that time Dick Grayson, the former Robin), and Starfire formed a new League in 2010 that he finally became a fully-fledged member. He formed a close bond with the android Red Tornado, helping to rebuild his badly damaged teammate, and acted in a reserve capacity in a number of adventures.

Then, in 2011, everything changed. As part of DC's "New 52" relaunch – wherein DC's history and characters were revised and recreated – Cyborg's origin was altered so that he became a founding member of the Justice League.

As before, Vic's transformation into Cyborg began in his father's lab; but in this retold origin, the accident that critically injured Vic came about as a result of an exploding Mother Box – an incredibly advanced device originating on the nightmarish world of Apokolips. With his son slipping away from him, Silas used nanites and technology accumulated from around the world to turn Vic into Cyborg. Now inextricably linked to the Apokoliptian energies of the Mother Box, Cyborg proved decisive in defeating Darkseid, Lord of Apokolips, and his invading Parademons.

Since then, Cyborg has been a fixture of the Justice League, his upgraded powers and abilities –

01
Cyborg as drawn by George Perez, who provided art for many of the New Teen Titans' most iconic stories. This 1982 issue showcased Cyborg's origin

02
Cyborg with the New Teen Titans from their 1985 debut issue. Here you can see him with then-regular members: Starfire, Kid Flash, Robin, Raven, Beast Boy, and Wonder Girl

03
Cyborg's solo *Rebirth* comic (2016)

04
Cyborg joins the big leagues – the Justice League! From 2012's *Justice League* #8

05 & 06
Cyborg had plenty of angst in his comics (*Tales of the New Teen Titans* #65 from 1986 and *Tales of the New Teen Titans: Cyborg* from 1982).

including the means to open Boom Tubes (teleportation tunnels), reconfigure himself to create different sorts of arm cannons, and absorb other technologies – proving a strong advantage to the team on countless occasions. Yet those self-same abilities have also sometimes left him open to attack. When the Crime Syndicate – evil doppelgängers of the Justice League hailing from a parallel Earth – launched an attack on the League, Cyborg's cybernetic systems were subverted. The machine elements of his body rejected and forcibly ejected the human parts, creating a nefarious consciousness named Grid. Though Vic – now outfitted in a sleek new Cyborg suit by his father – eventually took down Grid, the entity survived, lurking inside Cyborg's systems to emerge and ally once more with the Crime Syndicate. These episodes have only served to underline Vic's greatest fear: that he will one day lose his humanity completely, and become merely a machine. ◾

DELIVERING JUSTICE

If there's one group more powerful than the Justice League, then it's the team of producers who joined forces to oversee the League's debut movie. Here, Producers Charles Roven, Deborah Snyder, Jon Berg, and Geoff Johns join Executive Producers Wesley Coller and Curtis Kanemoto to discuss uniting the ultimate Super Hero team!

Justice League Collector's Edition:
How does this film pick up where
Batman v Superman left off? What's
the connection?
CHARLES ROVEN (Producer): It picks
up almost immediately after *Batman
v Superman*. As you recall, Lex Luthor
has told Batman that the bell has been
rung and that "he's hungry, he's found
us, and he's coming". This registers
with Bruce Wayne and he tells Diana
Prince that he feels that there's some
imminent type of attack coming.
Superman has died and left the planet
vulnerable, and Bruce knows that he's
got to find a team of metahumans to
help combat that threat.
WESLEY COLLER (Executive
Producer): It's a fun movie in the
sense that we get to watch this team
get built. We get to see Bruce find
inspiration in the sacrifice Superman
made, and it renews his faith in
humanity. It reminds Bruce what's
good about mankind.
DEBORAH SNYDER (Producer):
Batman v Superman is a deconstructive
look at the Super Heroes. *Justice League*
really builds up the Super Heroes.
JON BERG (Producer): Superman is
dead and the world is different – it's
without hope – and it needs defenders.
We need heroes. And Bruce knows he
needs to gather a team of metahumans.

How does it feel to be part of such
a huge, iconic project?
CURTIS KANEMOTO (Executive
Producer): It's a huge honor to bring
these larger-than-life characters to the
big screen together for the first time,

01
The team line
up on set

02
The cast surround
director Zack Snyder
as they watch a
scene on the monitor

03
The crew film a
scene on location
with Jason Momoa
as Aquaman

> ## EVERY SINGLE MEMBER OF THE JUSTICE LEAGUE IS A STAR IN THEIR OWN RIGHT. YOU'VE GOT TO MAKE SURE THAT THE AUDIENCE BECOMES INVESTED IN EACH ONE OF THEIR CHARACTER ARCS.

and to be able to tell that story of
how the team unites.
GEOFF JOHNS (Producer): I've
been waiting to see this film since I
was a kid. Actually, when I was a kid I
never dreamed we would get a *Justice
League* film. So for me, it's a lifelong
wish realized.
JON BERG: It's a dream. These are the
most iconic and legendary heroes on
the planet. To participate in realizing
them on film and uniting them in one
movie is a deep honor.
DEBORAH SNYDER: People have been
waiting for this for so many years. It's
so humbling and it's exhilarating to
finally get the chance to do it.
WESLEY COLLER: It's also cool that
we're getting to bring some additional
villains into our world. I don't want
to spoil it too much, but I think it's
always great to plant seeds. Our world
is expanding.

What were the biggest challenges
of creating this movie and how did
you face them?
CHARLES ROVEN: The biggest thing
about this movie is servicing the

number of characters, because every
single member of the Justice League is
a star in their own right. You've got to
make sure that the audience becomes
invested in each one of their character
arcs. The audience knows Wonder
Woman, Superman, Batman, but
not so much The Flash, Cyborg, and
Aquaman at this point.
JON BERG: It's a big, complex puzzle
piecing the film together. There's a ton
of costumes, VFX, stunts, characters,
sets, action, etc. It's a massive logistical
challenge, but a fun one.
WESLEY COLLER: It's about
knowing, respecting, and being
aware of the scale of the film. *Justice
League* is a bigger film than *Batman v
Superman*. There are more characters.
We see more of their world.
GEOFF JOHNS: There are a lot of
moving parts to this because we're
focused on a team of Super Heroes
that each stands alone. And there are a
lot of different worlds coming together
with them: Gotham, Metropolis,
Atlantis, Themyscira, Apokolips...

What is exciting about bringing
The Flash, Aquaman, and Cyborg
together into the mix?
JON BERG: It's so awesome seeing
them on screen together hanging out
and interacting. These are our modern
day gods and we get to play with them
and have them all together.
CURTIS KANEMOTO: You have
room to bring in more humor, and
also to have these moments of levity,
which is really interesting, because
Batman v Superman was about a battle
and, ultimately, death. *Justice League*
is a film about coming out of the ashes
and finding the chosen few to defend
the world.
   Wonder Woman and Batman
are a little bit older than the rest of
the League and they've seen a wider
gamut of humanity, both good and
bad. The dynamic between them
and the younger team members
allows for moments of humor and
competing perspectives.
GEOFF JOHNS: The interaction
between The Flash and Cyborg is
particularly fun. These two very
different characters, who have never ▶

01

> **"THE FLASH HAS BEEN FUN TO BRING TO LIFE. EZRA MILLER HAS TONS OF ENERGY AND A UNIQUE VOICE FOR THE CHARACTER. IT'S SO MUCH FUN TO SEE A NEW TAKE ON THE CHARACTER THAT WE HAVEN'T SEEN BEFORE."**

▶ been on the big screen before, coming together is a blast to watch. No one could be more enthusiastic about the team than Barry. And no one is more apprehensive about it than Victor. Well… except, maybe, for Arthur!

What are the team up against in this movie?

CURTIS KANEMOTO: Superman's death has awakened a Mother Box, which is an alien technology in the shape of a cube. One of these exists in man's world, one of these exists on Themyscira, and one in Atlantis. When one of these Mother Boxes awakens, it calls to Steppenwolf, our villain, and he arrives to collect them.

The story borrows from the world of Jack Kirby who created the New Gods. Zack Snyder, Geoff Johns and Chris Terrio have done an amazing job integrating all of the Apokoliptian tech in the world of the Justice League.

What can you tell us about the movie's villain, Steppenwolf?

CHARLES ROVEN: He's an alien determined to conquer the world. He comes from a pretty dark planet.

JON BERG: He's a warrior from another planet who tried to conquer Earth a few thousand years ago and failed. He's been living with the disgrace of having failed and desperately wants to avenge his previous loss.

What do you think the audience is going to like the most about this movie?

JON BERG: Hopefully, the camaraderie between them all. How they interrelate with one another and come together as the most dynamic team ever assembled.

WESLEY COLLER: Each one of the heroes is interesting, really cool, and has amazing abilities. To see them working in conjunction with one another is just that much more entertaining and fun to watch.

GEOFF JOHNS: My hope is that the fans of Batman, Superman and Wonder Woman become fans of The Flash, Cyborg and Aquaman. These are wonderful characters that mean a great deal to people and carry amazing messages and morality within them.

How does the team fit together?

WESLEY COLLER: The most entertaining part of the first act of the film is watching Bruce and Diana get on the same page after experiencing both successes and failures in their attempt to round up the team. It's fun to watch them try to wrap their heads around the psychology of each of these characters. Bruce's interaction with Barry Allen is quite comical and probably the easiest recruitment that's ever happened in the history of trying to get someone to join a team! On the other hand, Aquaman is not so keen on becoming part of the League!

What have the actors done to continue to breathe life into these characters?

CHARLES ROVEN: That's one of the great things about these stories having continuity from film to film. The characters progress and continue to expand and fulfill their arcs as the movies progress.

On *Man of Steel*, there was the arc of an orphan coming to grips with the fact that Earth was a place that he desperately wanted to become a part of and save. In *Batman v Superman*, he learned there was a cost to his saving the planet, and it was a cost that caused him to be alienated.

Bruce Wayne is a character who has lost his humanity. He's just seen too much darkness and been disappointed too many times. But he realizes, based on Superman's sacrifice, that there still are good men.

04
Early concept art for the film's main villain, Steppenwolf

05
Zack Snyder and the crew shoot a scene with Ezra Miller as The Flash

06
Filming Gal Gadot as Diana Prince

With Diana Prince, we're going to learn why she's laid low for the period of time that *Wonder Woman* takes place until where *Justice League* picks up and the true responsibility of being a hero. We'll learn more about Cyborg, Aquaman, and The Flash in *Justice League*. And then you'll see where their characters go in their own individual movies.

The heroes are all very powerful. Is it important to keep things relatable?

CHARLES ROVEN: Batman doesn't have any superpowers, so I find him relatable. A guy like The Flash does have superpowers, but he's so funny and vulnerable. He's lonely, even though he's the fastest man alive. He's dealing with loss in a really interesting way, and life's not perfect.

And Wonder Woman, for all of her majesty and being the Princess of Themyscira, and all of her warmth, she's also looking to find her place in man's world, but she's finding that challenging. She's beautiful, she's strong, she's immortal. Yet, she's also dealing with her own individual crises.

Who is your favorite Justice League member?

CURTIS KANEMOTO: The Flash has been fun to bring to life. Ezra

Miller has an enormous amount of energy and a unique voice for the character. It's incredibly entertaining to see his take on the character. It's really exciting to see where he's going to take the role, not only in Justice League but also in his standalone film.

JON BERG: I like them all equally and dig them individually. They are all the coolest characters in the universe – but I'm a little partial to the Flash.

CHARLES ROVEN: I started out reading *Detective Comics*, so obviously I'm a big fan of Batman.

DEBORAH SNYDER: I have an affinity for Wonder Woman, and The Flash is amazing too. Ezra is funny and charming, and it's a pleasure to watch him on the screen. And Ray Fisher as Cyborg, has real gravitas.

WESLEY COLLER: I like them all! But if I had to pick a favorite, I'd probably choose Cyborg. In our modern society, I think he's representative of the here and now in terms of all of our inner connectivity – our being wired all the time. He's most relevant to my personal existence and, what I see as the newest frontier. He has skills and abilities that make him something special in today's day and age.

GEOFF JOHNS: Growing up, my favorite character was The Flash. In many ways he still is. But at the

moment, I'd say Wonder Woman. To me, her film felt like *Superman: The Movie* – hopeful, iconic and impactful. It's been a long, long time since I felt that. And I love that we're seeing Diana back in theaters so quickly.

What can you tell us about *Justice League*'s great supporting characters?

CHARLES ROVEN: We have some talented actors, both returning and new, including: Amy Adams as Lois Lane, Diane Lane as Martha Kent, Jeremy Irons as Alfred, J.K. Simmons as Commissioner Gordon, and Billy Crudup as Henry Allen (Barry's father). It's great to have great actors playing these iconic characters, because it makes them feel very real.

WESLEY COLLER: J.K. Simmons takes on the role of Commissioner Gordon in a way that is a lot of fun to watch. He's got such an interesting relationship with Batman. Outside of Alfred, there's no one else that has that connectivity with him as that character.

DEBORAH SNYDER: We were so happy to be able to get J.K. to do this role. It was really important to him when he was doing the research on the character to look like the comics. So he has this amazing wig that ▶

> ## "THE JUSTICE LEAGUE STORY IS ABOUT THE FACT THAT IT'S NEVER TOO LATE TO REINVENT YOURSELF. IT'S NEVER TOO LATE TO GO BACK AND REEXAMINE THE PATH YOU'VE BEEN DOWN OR THINK ABOUT THINGS IN A DIFFERENT WAY. "

07
The Justice League pose with honorary members Zack Snyder (left), Charles Roven (middle), and DC President & Chief Creative Officer Geoff Johns (right)

08
Shooting a scene with the Amazons

09
Shooting a fiery sequence with Batman and the Batmobile

The *Justice League* production team includes: Wesley Coller (**10**), Deborah Snyder (**11**), Charles Roven (**12**), Curtis Kanemoto (**13**), Jon Berg (**14**), and Geoff Johns (**15**)

▶ looks right out of the comics, and a mustache.

WESLEY COLLER: It's great to have Jeremy Irons back as Alfred, because he's such a key component of who Bruce Wayne is. Alfred's disdain for the choices that Bruce is making and his ability to express fatherly discontent with some of Bruce's tactics is important. But also there's never a sense that he would ever abandon him. He's constantly testing Bruce. He's constantly asking the questions. And I think that it's his investment in Bruce that ultimately allows Bruce to excel at the level he does as Batman.

Billy Crudup, who plays The Flash's father, is probably one of my favorite actors of all time. I've never laughed as much between sets as I do when he's here. He and Ezra could be a comedy duo. The dynamic between them as they sit on opposite sides of the glass in the prison visiting room, and he expresses his hopes for his son and Barry shares his sorrow for the current situation of his father, is so genuine and interesting. It brings a layer of complexity to Barry's backstory.

DEBORAH SNYDER: Martha and Lois are Clark's connection to humanity and the way that he was connected to this planet. Martha goes through a lot because she's a proud woman. She actually loses her house, but she's too afraid to say anything to anybody, and Lois makes this transformation throughout the movie as well.

GEOFF JOHNS: One of the most emotional stories we follow is Lois Lane's, played by Amy Adams. Lois is one of the strongest and most driven characters in the DC Universe. So for us to see her dealing with the loss of Clark, to see how it effects her, is incredibly powerful.

WESLEY COLLER: Whether it's introducing Mera, or whether we're talking about beginning to understand the relationship between Barry and his father and what their past consists of – it's great to start laying the foundation for additional layers of these characters' existence.

What can you tell us about the world of the Justice League?

DEBORAH SNYDER: We get to see where the Justice League gets together in the Batcave. And it's pretty slick.

CURTIS KANEMOTO: We built the Batcave in *Batman v Superman*, and our visual effects team scanned the entire set so that we could recreate it later on digitally.

We get to explore S.T.A.R. Labs, a research lab that the government brought inside of the containment center in Metropolis to study the Kryptonian scout ship that crashed there in *Man of Steel*. This is where we get to meet Silas Stone, who is the head scientist at S.T.A.R. Labs. We also get to establish Central City, which is where Barry Allen is from.

We get to highlight some of the amazing locations in London, and we built some enormous sets on the stages and backlot of Warner Bros. Studio Leavesden.

Who would you want to be next to you in a fight?

CURTIS KANEMOTO: Definitely Wonder Woman, without a doubt. You do not want to mess with Wonder Woman because she's seen a lot in her lifetime, and she has no time to mess around.

But Superman's pretty amazing too. He's a pretty good ally to have on your side. So, I would probably say Superman.

CHARLES ROVEN: That's a tough one. I think you've probably got to say Superman.

WESLEY COLLER: Wonder Woman. I feel like anyone who is actually a half-god is worth having on your side!

DEBORAH SNYDER: I think Jason Momoa definitely has the biggest presence on the screen. He's so manly! I don't think we've ever seen an Aquaman like Jason's Aquaman.

How would you sum this movie up?

WESLEY COLLER: I think the Justice League story is about the fact that it's never too late. It's never too late to reinvent yourself, it's never too late to go back and reexamine the path you've been down. It's never too late to think about things in a different way, or to change the lens which you're seeing the world through.

CHARLES ROVEN: It's about the challenge of bringing this disparate group together and seeing whether or not they can actually find a way to work together to defeat the threat. And also, are they going to do it in a way that will give them a reason to continue to work together? ▰

07

08

09

13

14

15

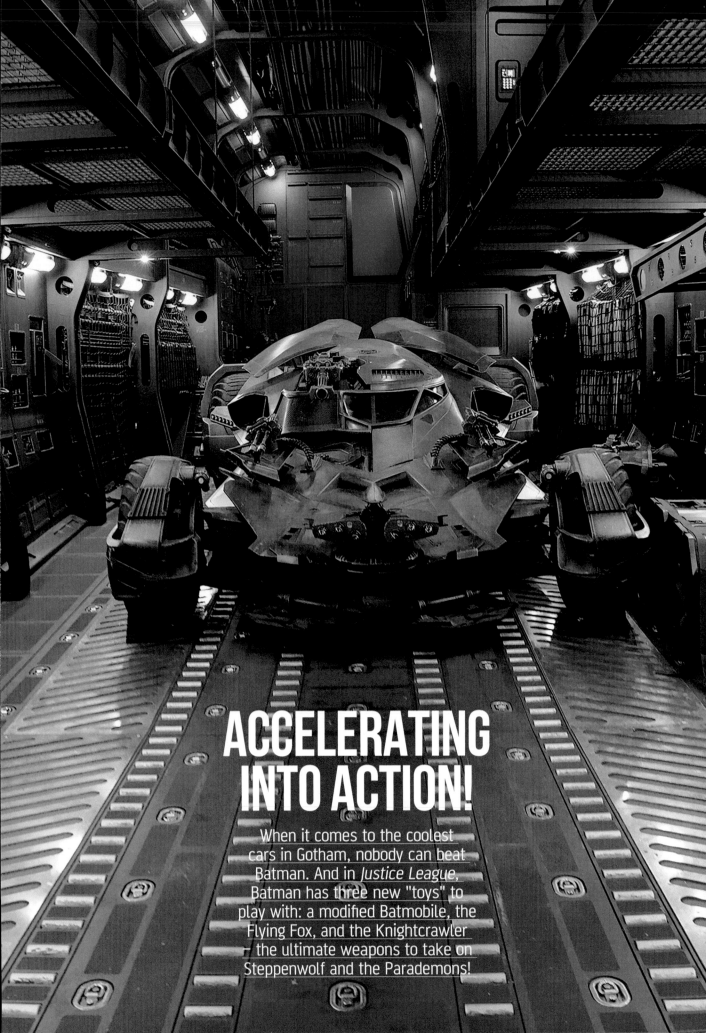

ACCELERATING INTO ACTION!

When it comes to the coolest cars in Gotham, nobody can beat Batman. And in *Justice League*, Batman has three new "toys" to play with: a modified Batmobile, the Flying Fox, and the Knightcrawler – the ultimate weapons to take on Steppenwolf and the Parademons!

THE BATMOBILE

Executive Producer,
CURTIS KANEMOTO:
"In *Batman v Superman*, the Batmobile was damaged by Superman, so Bruce Wayne has upgraded it in *Justice League*. He has added some additional armaments and some cool new features."

Production Designer,
PATRICK TATOPOULOS:
"In every movie there's a singular object that defines the aesthetic of the film. In *Batman v Superman*, the Batmobile was that for me.

"We didn't want to reinvent the Batmobile completely. It has always been designed in a way that it looked like it could be changed or upgraded. With this version, we wanted it to feel like Batman is going to war. The weaponry is being loaded to the max. And it's interesting how different the car looks. It's not just a Batmobile anymore; it's a Batmobile tank.

"Past Batmobiles have done a lot of jumping and landing over the years, but when they land, because their suspension is meant to be low, they smash the ground, which doesn't look elegant. I wanted a car that can jump and look like an off-road car. I'm mad about motorcycles and when I get a car to design, I bring a lot of motorycle stuff to the process. The whole suspension system of the Batmobile is very much based on how a motorcycle works.

"There are other modifications; the passenger seat is gone. I put the cannon there and two machine guns on the top. There are more missile launchers on the back. The new guns on the Batmobile are inspired by real weapons. We were inspired by top-of-the-line new weaponry on the market and matched it. So what you see on the car are not fantasy weapons.

"Things like the Batmobile are so iconic that it creates pressure when you design your version. I'm a fan too!"

Above: The work-in-progress Batmobile being upgraded and the armored Batmobile in action

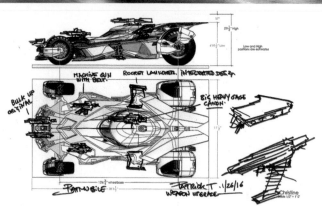

Above: Early upgraded Batmobile sketches by Production Designer Patrick Tatopoulos

The enormous Flying Fox in the Bat Hangar

THE FLYING FOX

Production Designer,
PATRICK TATOPOULOS:
"On every movie I make, there are certain things that really get me pumped up: the Flying Fox was something that I really got excited about because it was a chance for us to create a really exciting new airplane. I wanted it to look like a jet.

"The Flying Fox is a gigantic plane and the Batmobile fits inside – so you can see that the scale of that plane is incredibly big. I tackled that plane before anything else on the film. Unfortunately, it's a vehicle that we would never actually build because of the scale of it, so you only see part of it. In some ways, I wish there were no computers so we had to build it! As a designer, you want to build things like that.

"When you think of a bomber airplane, it seems like there's a cockpit in the front like a commercial airplane. I started to design the plane with the cockpit in the front, but then I took the plane's cockpit and slid it all the way to the back. I used my interest in Spitfires and Second World War fighter jets as inspiration for the Flying Fox.

"When I was in Detroit working on *Batman v Superman*, I saw a steam engine from the 1930s. It was incredible, with pipes everywhere, and looked really cool and old. It had been painted multiple times with this weird paint. It was like this weird organic thing. I decided to make the walls of the Flying Fox look like that and I was really pleased with the end result."

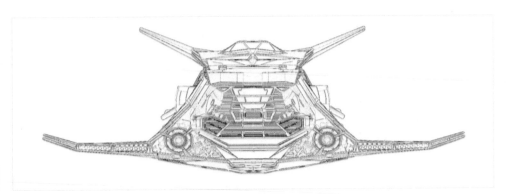

Right: Detailed concept sketch of the Flying Fox

Below: Batman's Flying Fox proves very handy for the League

Executive Producer, **CURTIS KANEMOTO:** "The Flying Fox is a craft that can house the Justice League and it can also house the Batmobile! When I saw the concept art, I thought, okay, that's awesome. I want one of those."

Above: The League enter the Flying Fox in this concept painting

Early sketch of the Knightcrawler (below left) and a developed piece of concept art (below right)

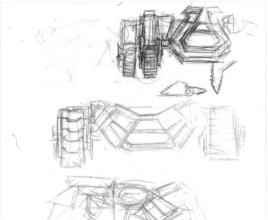

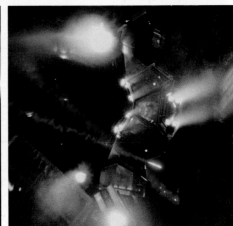

Above: The Knightcrawler in action

Executive Producer, **CURTIS KANEMOTO:**
"Batman always needs to have some type of awesome tech and in this movie, we introduce the Knightcrawler. This is an amazing four-legged tank-like vehicle that can house several members of the Justice League. It can also climb walls and has articulating arms. It's something every kid can only dream of!"

THE
KNIGHTCRAWLER

Production Designer, **PATRICK TATOPOULOS:**
"For long distances, the Knightcrawler wasn't very practical, so I decided to have tank-like treads living within its legs. The whole cockpit is built practically, but the actual legs and all the moving parts were computer-generated.

"I asked myself, how does it climb walls? I decided that it has spikes on the side of the legs that embed themselves in the wall and widen, so they get stuck there, and then the other one goes, and the first one retracts and comes out. So you have this kind of crazy language where every time a leg goes on the wall, it pulls out 12 bricks or something like that.

"When we first discussed it, I was worried it was too far into the realm of science fiction. However, I was wrong, because, as it developed, it all came together and became a vehicle that was a believable part of Batman's world."

BRUCE &
DIANA'S
WHEELS

Executive Producer,
WESLEY COLLER:
"Mercedes have been a great partner for us in this movie and they've given us access to new and exciting vehicles that people will actually be able to buy. There are very few companies in the world that could deliver a product that's worthy of being part of Bruce Wayne's fleet.

"We had the opportunity in the film to put Diana in the new, yet-to-be-seen E-Class Mercedes-Benz, which is a beautiful sedan. It's very fitting of what I feel Diana Prince would drive."

Above: Bruce Wayne's AMG Vision Gran Turismo and Diana Prince's E-Class provided by Mercedes-Benz

SUPER HERO STYLE

Costume Designer Michael Wilkinson has faced many creative challenges in his career, but *Justice League* provided his biggest challenges yet! Here Michael discusses how he helped the team look super-cool...

Costume designer Michael Wilkinson has a huge amount of experience in his craft, having worked over the last two decades on such diverse films as *300, Watchmen, Twilight, Noah,* and *American Hustle,* but *Justice League* posed challenges of its own. "This film is hands-down the largest scale film I've ever worked on," Wilkinson tells us.

And he's not exaggerating. Wilkinson and his team faced a 25-week shoot, with 3,000 extras to costume, plus having to create multiple versions of hero costumes for the main actors for their many fight scenes. "In *Batman v Superman,* we had Superman, Batman, and we introduced Wonder Woman. We teased some of the new characters, but in *Justice League* we really explore each of their separate universes and backstories, so we're making a lot more costumes this time around. But we love a challenge...

"We do lots of research into how these characters have been portrayed over the decades," Wilkinson continues. "We love these characters, and we care about portraying them in a way that is relevant to

today's audiences, but also respects their history."

For this movie, Michael Wilkinson and his costume department were based at Warner Bros. Studio Leavesden in the UK. "I have an incredible team of costumers," Wilkinson says. "We have the people that illustrate the concept art and the team that manage the workroom. There are people that create these incredible fabrics, that make the molds that cast out all of these pieces, and the guys who glue them down. There's the team that do all of the art finishing and the incredible paintwork. It really takes an army to assemble these costumes!"

Getting it right is very important to Wilkinson and his team. "In this kind of Super Hero film, the audience really likes to see very well thought-out, detailed costumes," he says. "It's an amazing opportunity for a costume designer to have the time and the resources to do all of this research and development – in order to create things that audiences haven't seen before. Hopefully the results will be spectacular!"

Over the next few pages, we take a look at some of Wilkinson's thought processes on how he and his talented team developed the costumes of the *Justice League* characters...

This page: Detail on Batman's costume and cowl

BATMAN

Michael Wilkinson: "There's always the opportunity to reinvent Batman's costumes. There are technologies that weren't available last time around, and you just want to make it better and better.

"We wanted to bring things back to basics and really honor how you see this character in the comic books. We wanted it to feel like he's been fighting crime for a long time.

"Along with the regular suit, we also get to see what we call the tactical suit. From our very first *Justice League* meeting, we talked about having a suit where Batman really steps up his look for the third act. He knows he's gonna go in for a fight with the ultimate threat, so he and Alfred work on the tactical suit. There's a whole layer of protective armor that goes on top of our classic Batsuit.

"We made about eight versions of each suit for this film. It was super challenging to make the costumes comfortable and not too hot, and also Ben Affleck had to be able to do all of the moves too.

"One of the joys for me for doing these films is working out the Super Hero looks versus civilian looks, and to make subtle connections between the two. So the color palette of Bruce Wayne is quite similar to the Batsuit – lots of steely grays. He's very austere in the way he dresses. His clothes are incredibly expensive and beautifully made but they're not at all flashy."

This page: Detail on Wonder Woman's battle-ready costume, including the torso armor, shield and sword, and the 'WW' belt

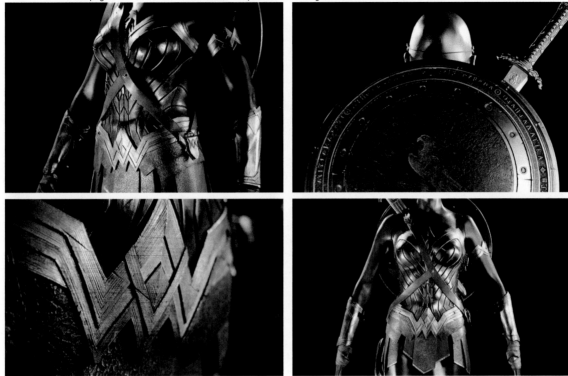

WONDER WOMAN

Michael Wilkinson: "I really enjoyed working on Wonder Woman's costume because she's such an important Super Hero. She's the first really big, iconic female Super Hero. And it was so important for us to really get it right and to get the balance of strength, grace, majesty, and badass.

"Of course, before *Justice League* you have the *Wonder Woman* stand-alone film, which has costume design by Lindy Hemming. Lindy and I got together in 2015 and spent a couple of weeks researching the world of *Wonder Woman* and coming up with a visual language for the character and her world. There was a great crossover between the films that she and I worked on.

"Wonder Woman is a joy to dress. In our film, she works at the Louvre and she's an incredibly switched-on expert in antiquities. Diana has a very cosmopolitan, fashion forward look.

"I knew I had to include all of the iconic details of the costume. Someone might look at her costume and think it's relatively simple – it's not! Her choices of leathers, her colors, some of the lashing and lacing details that I put into her civilian wear, they all have a crossover with the Amazonian look. Her costume has changed a little since *Batman v Superman*. It's a bit more vibrant and colorful this time around and has a little bit more glow to it."

A selection of Diana's fashions as created by Costume Designer Michael Wilkinson

CYBORG

Michael Wilkinson: "Even though Cyborg was a majority CG character, we did a full exploration of his look, just as though we were going to build it. We did illustrations of all different views and we explored different textures. I'm all about textures and layering and colors – it's really important to me. It was great just to think about technologies that weren't human – the mechanical joints and connections that are unknown to us. And his silhouette was a really exciting thing for us to explore – the way that his shape can grow and diminish and can build shapes and transform within his form.

"I worked with my concept artist to create lots of different artwork to inspire what the final look for Cyborg might be. At a certain point we handed it over to the visual effects department and they kept developing the look with the director and with the actor's performance. So they're creating his final look in the computer.

"Victor Stone has a really interesting style too. Before his accident, we really wanted to feel that he had a sense of promise and a purity. He has a classic clean-cut American-style collegiate, sporty kind of look. When we see him then transformed into this intimidating metallic creature, then that contrast is really felt. We really wanted to portray the tragedy of his story."

Below: The full Cyborg look; Above: The man behind the mecha – Ray Fisher

Creating The Flash
01 Costume Designer Michael Wilkinson sketching on the set of Barry's apartment
02 Sketches of The Flash's outfit for set decoration
03 Members of the team work on The Flash's costume
04 Sketches and parts of The Flash's costume for set decoration
05 The final results on set!

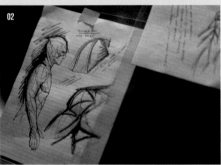

Below: Details of The Flash's costume as created by Michael Wilkinson and his team

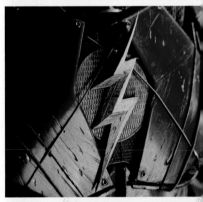

THE FLASH

Michael Wilkinson: "This is the beginning of The Flash's story, and so it was important for us to set up his world. Barry is much younger than some of the other guys and he's a bit of a joker. I really wanted to get that young, generational thing going with the way he dresses.

"His clothing is quite different to his teammates' – it's a very layered street-skater/punk feel. He wears hoodies and flannel shirts and skinny pants. Ezra was lots of fun to dress. He's such an interesting guy and brings a lot of ideas to the table.

"Barry has got the skater punk feel to him but he's also extremely intelligent and he's great with technology. We were thinking about what look he would come up with to try and deal with these new powers – something to protect himself from the high speeds that he's traveling at and the huge temperatures that he would be exposed to. We thought: what would Barry do? Well, he would go online, he would research what NASA is doing, he would go and get a 3D printer.

"And so his costume has that fantastic blend of high technologies such as heat-resistant materials, prototypes and aerodynamic shapes... He might have explored vehicle design and plane design and how things move through space very quickly. But it's all mixed with a great grassroots, distressed aesthetic. Zack [Snyder] really wanted it to feel like a prototype suit. This is the very first manifestation of Barry putting together a look."

Above: The full Aquaman costume – complete with trident

AQUAMAN

Michael Wilkinson: "I was really excited about diving – if you pardon the pun – into the Atlantean world. It's such a fantastic culture and we came up with our own graphic language of motifs and applied it to the Atlantean costumes. We researched and read the comics to make sure we were being faithful to the legacy of the Atlanteans.

"Aquaman is the first glimpse we have into the whole Atlantean culture, and so we took it upon ourselves to really try to express his culture in the suit – in the scales and the beautiful ritualistic linework that goes through the costume. You also see it repeated in the production design's architectural motifs, and the whole visual world that we're building for Atlantis in this film.

"Sometimes when he begins to undress, we get a look at those amazing tattoos, and there's a real correlation between the tattoos and the Aquaman suit.

"Jason Momoa is such a fun guy to dress. He has such a great sense of clothes and style. He really brought a lot to the table as we were coming up with a look for Arthur Curry. We wanted a salty, maritime look to him with foul weather gear. Aquaman was always around the sea but still had a rock 'n' roll, bad boy kind of look. He is lots of fun."

Above: The beautiful detail on Aquaman's costume; Top: Jason Momoa as Arthur Curry/Aquaman

Above: The full Superman costume plus some of the intricate detail. Detail of the "S" symbol, belt, and cuffs showing elements of the Kryptonian language

SUPERMAN

Michael Wilkinson: "It's interesting thinking about the journey Superman's costume took. It has appeared in three films now. In the first one, *Man of Steel*, the costume was actually started off by amazing costume designer Jim Acheson. I took over on that film and developed some of the details further.

"When we got to *Batman v Superman*, we were able to streamline and tweak the details. To get a third chance to work on the costume in *Justice League* was a dream come true. In *Batman v Superman*, the colors were quite muted. We decided to make the colors more saturated in *Justice League*.

"Zack Snyder had the fantastic idea of incorporating some Kryptonian scripts through the suit. We weaved some Kryptonian language through the 'S', across the bicep, through the belt and the cuff details. So they add that extra layer of meaning and detail for the audience.

"We developed an extremely beautiful metallic-chromed undersuit for Henry Cavill. He wears a slightly bolder blue than the last film, so he jumps off the screen in such a heroic way.

"Since the first film, we've found fabrics that are even more sheer and beautiful and lustrous, but they are also super strong and they don't fall apart when they're stretched tightly over Henry's body.

"So all of these little tiny tweaks add up to a bigger, stronger costume."

03

CHRISTIAN SCHEURER

01 Early concept art of Atlanteans guarding the Mother Box

02 Concept painting of Aquaman with his trident

03 Aquaman in his natural environment

AQUAMAN'S WORLD

While Batman, Superman, and Wonder Woman are now familiar faces on the big screen, some of the *Justice League* team members and their origins are still being established. But that's not a problem, because it gave the creative geniuses behind the movie the chance to explore, create and flesh out the worlds and universes of characters like Cyborg, The Flash and Aquaman.

Here, we take a look at some of the designs and thought processes that went into the creation of the world of Arthur Curry – a.k.a. Aquaman. ▶

PRODUCTION DESIGNER
PATRICK TATOPOULOS ON
AQUAMAN'S WORLD

"I like Aquaman because his world is completely created from scratch – and it's huge. He comes from a world of creatures, and I find that fascinating and exciting. I designed creatures in the first part of my career and I've always been interested in humans and creatures being mixed together.

"First of all, we needed to establish an aesthetic for Aquaman's world. It's very stark – it's not organic. It's not what you would expect for Aquaman. There's a city that used to be on the surface, and it's down underwater now. My thought was that maybe the world exists in crevasses. The city has slid like a deck of cards.

"There are six different Justice League characters that each need to have their own different world. You want to easily go, 'I'm underwater now – I'm here in Aquaman's world.' You need to define that look by creating little elements of it.

"You'll get to see a lot more of Aquaman's world in his stand-alone movie in 2018!"

01

02

03

04

05

01
Jason Momoa as Aquaman

02
A sketch of the underwater Mother Box

03
A fleshed-out concept painting of the Mother Box in the Atlantean Stronghold

04
Aquaman emerges from his world

05
Concept painting showing another viewpoint of the Mother Box area

Amber Heard as Mera plus concept art and costume development for her character

COSTUME DESIGNER **MICHAEL WILKINSON** ON

MERA'S LOOK

"Mera, the female lead of Atlantis, was a fantastic character for me to work on. What I love about her is that she's such a badass warrior. We really wanted her costume to resemble armor. It's a protective look but with an interesting amphibious, underwater quality to it. We researched fish scales and textures which used bioluminescence, to come up with her costume design. There's some amazing engineering and architecture that goes into maintaining her very stylized and unique aesthetic."

CYBORG'S WORLD

Creating the look for a mostly-CG character provided an interesting challenge for the *Justice League* movie's creative team. Here, some key members of the crew reveal their thoughts on the character...

Production Designer,
PATRICK TATOPOULOS:

"Cyborg's world is about science and high tech. He's embedded with technology after his accident. It's a whole other look. He is different to the other characters. In essence, Cyborg's costume barely existed when we were filming. It's designed, but it's computer-generated."

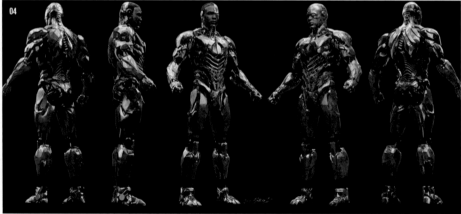

Producer,
CHARLES ROVEN:

"Cyborg has a really interesting journey, because he has to come to grips with whether or not he would rather be dead. Is he actually alive? Does the human part of him still exist? He's created from the same alien technology that created the Parademons, and Patrick Tatopoulos has used similar design cues. There's more conflict with his character as he doesn't have full control over his body, which we get to play with in the film in an intriguing way."

01
Cyborg concept sketch by Costume Designer Michael Wilkinson

02
Cyborg in full effect

03
Close-up of Cyborg's torso

04
More developed designs by Michael Wilkinson and his team

05
Concept painting for Cyborg

06
Cyborg holds a Mother Box

07
Cyborg as he appears in the *Justice League* movie

Executive Producer, **CURTIS KANEMOTO**: "Ray Fisher brings such a unique take on Cyborg. He has such a great personality and brings great energy to everything that we ask of him."

BARRY'S PAD

Production Designer Patrick Tatopoulos guides us through the development of The Flash's eye-popping world...

Creating designs for The Flash posed an exciting challenge for the *Justice League*'s creative teams. Here, Production Designer Patrick Tatopoulos – in his own words – describes exactly how he and his team faced that challenge...

Starting points...
Patrick Tatopoulos: "This is a set unlike anything I've done before. It's so colorful, so funky and so crazy, and it balances greatly with the other characters – but it's totally different.

"What became clear to me is that there is the world of Batman, the world of Superman, the world of Aquaman, the world of Wonder Woman, and the world of Cyborg – five different characters in this movie that have their own elements, who create their own specific worlds with different colors and different textures.

"Then we got to The Flash and he's the young kid on the block, so he ▶

06

07

> **"I THOUGHT THE FLASH'S WORLD SHOULD BE COLORFUL. I CAN'T TELL YOU HOW COOL IT WAS TO JUMP IN THERE AND EMBRACE ALL THE COLORS. IT'S CRAZY, AND THAT'S REFRESHING."**

▶ had to bring something different to the other Super Heroes. We had to explore what's cool for the young generation today. And also, he's a messy kid! So the ideas started with this."

The Flash's colors...
Patrick Tatopoulos: "Color-wise, we thought, 'why don't we make this a guy that's just all over the place?' He's very eclectic. Batman's color palette is a dark gray and with Wonder Woman we're playing with two colors. I thought The Flash's world should be the opposite of that – it should be colorful. I can't tell you how cool it was to jump in there and embrace all the colors. I actually don't think there's a color palette. It's crazy, and that's refreshing.

"Of course, The Flash is red and gold and we could have gone in that direction with the character. But when you get the chance to create characters that are not immortal or alien, and you have some characters that feel a bit more grounded in reality, you've got to use that. Bruce Wayne is a man who's got money and power. The Flash is not like that, and when you explore and play with that it's a good thing for the audience to relate to."

The concepts...
Patrick Tatopoulos: "The Flash's loft is interesting, because we were looking at locations in Los Angeles and I found a couple of places that were quite grungy, but also stylish and interesting.

"The biggest concept that I was playing with is the idea that there are hundreds of screens in his room. I had been thinking that would be great because he has all this electricity in him. Some of the screens are modern and some are old. And when he turns them on, the screens don't all open at once... and we reveal the room with the screen lights slowly turning on.

"Barry also recycled an old couch – it's next to the most hi-tech computer. I love that mismatch of having a young geek creating his world like that. I got a lot of inspiration from a couple of

friends of mine who are computer geeks and they love extreme sports. That's the way this has been set up. It's a bit messy, but it's also very techy. You can get so much inspiration from the people you know.

"We used duct tape to colorize the pipes in his apartment, because that's what Barry would have done. We were like, 'we're The Flash, and we're gonna go in there and paint', and we had a great time!"

Ezra Miller...
Patrick Tatopoulos: "Ezra got really involved in the design. I love when actors come and talk to you and say, 'Hey, could we have this? Could we have that?' When I did *I, Robot* with Will Smith, it was the same thing. Will got very involved in designing his apartment, and to me, that's phenomenal. On a few movies, you get the actors actually going to their set the day before and they just hang out on their own, just to get a feel for the place. I love that. Commitment is great and it's a fun way to work with actors."

Working on the pad...
Patrick Tatopoulos: "The day we shot in Barry's apartment, the crew were all happy and in a good mood. There was definitely something fun and positive and goofy about that place. Ezra really loved it too, and he felt very connected to the set. It's nice when you hear that. When you walk in there and you see the actors responding well, it's very important.

"Yesterday, we shot from the inside of the most high tech jet. That's Bruce Wayne's man cave. Well this is Barry's funky man cave! It's great when you jump from one set like that to the other.

"So that was the concept for The Flash. The concept was not so much about what the space is, it's what the mess in the space is. It's been a lot of fun creating him. We went to town with it – and that's kind of refreshing." ◗

01 Barry gets a mysterious visitor...

02 Behind the scenes with Ben Affleck on the set of The Flash's pad

03 Barry examines a batarang

04 Barry's prototype suit in his apartment

05 Colors and chaos – those are the themes of Barry's apartment

06 A familiar mask

07 Screens are a big part of the apartment's design

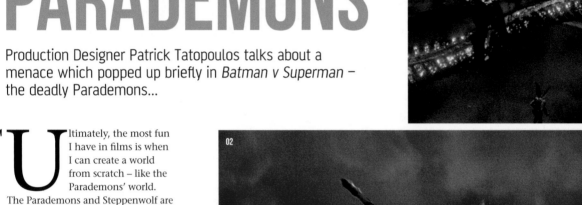

THE PARADEMONS

Production Designer Patrick Tatopoulos talks about a menace which popped up briefly in *Batman v Superman* – the deadly Parademons...

"Ultimately, the most fun I have in films is when I can create a world from scratch – like the Parademons' world. The Parademons and Steppenwolf are based in this abandoned nuclear plant in Russia. Once Steppenwolf unleashes his alien tech, it begins to transform into his world, like a cancer living in this abandoned power plant.

"These guys are alien, but their look has a mix of elements – technological, organic and mechanical. They're clearly a different species.

"It was important that our evil characters are not just typical dark gray things – so we have come up with colors for them. I'm excited because we've created really evil characters, but they look different.

"Designing villains is challenging because you don't want to repeat things you've seen in the past. We want to bring something that's fresh and new. Most of it will be CGI but I usually end up spending more time designing these kinds of worlds and characters. It's like being a kid every day... I love designing monsters!"

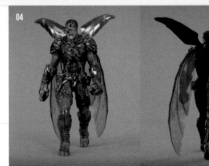

01
Film frame of
Steppenwolf and
his Parademons
preparing for battle

02
Aquaman surfs
a Parademon

03
Sketches of
Parademons' weapons

04
CGI shot of a
Parademon

05
The Parademons
attack the Batmobile

06
A concept sketch
showing the JL
team fighting the
Parademons

07
CG rendering of
a battle-ready
Parademon

08
Detailed concept
sketch of a Parademon
by Patrick Tatopoulos

WELCOME TO GOTHAM

Production Designer Patrick Tatopoulos and Director of Photography Fabian Wagner discuss elements of some of *Justice League*'s iconic Gotham scenes...

Think of Batman and many things come to mind – Alfred, the Batcave, the Batmobile, and so on. But one thing set to give fans chills is the Gotham City Police Department rooftop sequence in *Justice League*. In these scenes, Commissioner Jim Gordon (played by J.K. Simmons) lights up the famous Bat-Signal and meets up with the Dark Knight himself – plus a few friends.

Members of the film's creative team reveal how they approached this sequence, their thought processes behind the designs – and just where they got that Bat-Signal from...

THE GCPD ROOFTOPS

Production Designer,
PATRICK TATOPOULOS:
"In every film, some of the sets are *really* exciting to work on. The Justice League team's Hangar was a big deal for me, and the GCPD rooftop was also something that I was very passionate about.

"You want Gotham to be a place that people can recognize instantly, and the GCPD rooftop scene definitely does that. There's an iconic moment where we have Batman – his cape flowing – standing up on a Gotham rooftop on a gargoyle, and that's an image I'm hoping that the audience will really connect with. It's only there for three or four seconds, but it's a major thing. It's a poster you want on your bedroom wall as a kid, and it's one of those moments where you are reminded that you're working on this crazy, amazing Super Hero film.

"I'd sketched the rooftop and then I went on to sketch the gargoyle. Rather than creating an ugly or cartoony gargoyle, I wanted it to be a beautiful creature. I felt it needed to be turn-of-the-century and realistic – something that's got a darkness to it. Gargoyles are great – you can always see something new when you look at them from a different angle. It had to be massive, because that would be really ridiculous to have this big, strong Batman sitting on this tiny little gargoyle.

"The gargoyles and statues have turned out the way I was dreaming they would turn out. They're hand-made and they are fantastic. We spent a lot of time on those with the sculptors. It's great when you're able to build and create something, away from the CGI – it's great to make something palpable, where you can feel grounded."

"

THE GOTHAM ROOFTOP WAS ALSO SOMETHING THAT I WAS VERY PASSIONATE ABOUT. YOU WANT GOTHAM TO BE A PLACE THAT PEOPLE CAN RECOGNIZE INSTANTLY, AND THE GOTHAM ROOFTOP SCENE DEFINITELY DOES THAT.

"

Director of Photography,
FABIAN WAGNER:
"The Bat-Signal is so iconic. It's amazing. I never thought I'd be shooting the Bat-Signal in a million years.

"Back in the US there are around 1500 of these lights, but in England, this is the only one left that we could track down. We were lucky that the owner of that light allowed us to paint it!"

THE BAT-SIGNAL

Production Designer,
PATRICK TATOPOULOS:
"The light we got is old but it still looks good. We painted it the Batman gray, the color scheme which was defined on the last film. It's cool when it's turned on. I've seen a lot of simple Bat-Signals, but I love the technology going on with this one."

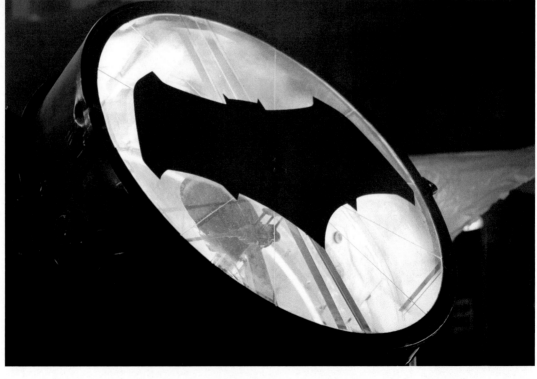

HENRY CAVILL IS

SUPERMAN

The world is in mourning as this once-feared Kryptonian is now seemingly forever silenced after sacrificing himself to save mankind. Inspired by the Man of Steel, the Justice League comes together to represent his sense of eternal hope.

Justice League Collector's Edition: You're back as the Man of Steel for the third time. How did you feel, slipping into Superman's costume again?
Henry Cavill: Putting the suit on was fantastic. I love wearing that suit. No matter how warm or uncomfortable it gets, it's the Superman suit. There's no feeling like it. It's a truly unique, special thing, and I hope I get to do it for many more years. I'm really happy.

Do you continue to immerse yourself in the world of the comics?
I do indeed – especially with *Rebirth*, which has just come out. I've been really diving into that. It's fun to see where the DC Comics Universe is going, and to see how closely our movie universe is matching it.

Have you been working closely with DC President & Chief Creative Officer Geoff Johns to really get into your character?
Geoff and I have been delving into the history of the character to get to the core of who Superman is.

The *Daily Planet* reports on a world without Superman

BIO

Henry Cavill was born on the Channel Island of Jersey. He started his acting career at the age of 18 in the film *Laguna* and quickly followed that up with roles in TV and film, including *The Count of Monte Cristo, Midsomer Murders,* and *The Inspector Lynley Mysteries*. In 2003, he had his first supporting role in the film *I Capture the Castle*, which he followed up with roles in *Hellraiser: Hellworld, Red Riding Hood, Tristan & Isolde,* and *Stardust*. In 2007, he landed his first leading role in the Emmy Award-winning TV show *The Tudors*, and in 2013 he gained international fame thanks to his iconic portrayal of Superman. Away from the camera, Cavill is a spokesman for the Durrell Wildlife Conservation Trust, and an ambassador for The Royal Marines Charity.

What role does Lois Lane fulfill for Superman?
I think Lois was, and is, a true anchor for Superman, and she always has been.

How do you think Lois and Martha have been affected by Clark Kent's absence?
They were sure that he and Superman were dead and gone. It must have been excruciating for both Martha and Lois to be there and see all these people mourning this Super Hero who none of them truly knew.

How does Superman fit into the Justice League?
It's much like the United States with the League of Nations. Without that keystone, the Justice League doesn't really work. It's still a fantastic group of people, but Superman tends to be the heavy hitter of the League. He sometimes takes a leadership role, but most of the time it's Batman who takes a leadership role. Superman is more the moral compass for the League.

What is it like to see the Justice League all suited up?
It's very, very surreal. This is a wonderful job. I love my job, especially when I'm playing Superman, but sometimes you do start to feel the wear and tear of a long day. There was one point where I was standing in one of the huge green screen sets – which can be quite draining in itself, because it's a very bright, aggressive green – and I was

▶

▶ standing there at the top of these big stairs, thinking how hungry I am, and looking forward to getting to bed... And then I had this moment when I suddenly realized that Cyborg, Aquaman, and Wonder Woman were all standing there, and it looked so fantastic. All of a sudden, my tiredness slipped away. I wasn't hungry any more. I just wanted to live in this moment and remember that I'm doing the thing that I wanted to do as a kid. I'm essentially playing Super Heroes, but as real as it gets as an adult. I'm very thankful for that kind of thing.

How would you describe your fellow Justice League members?
Gal Gadot is fantastic as Wonder Woman. We've got Ray Fisher who is great as Cyborg. He creates a great energy on set, and brings that character to life in such a great way – I think he's really going to make his mark on that character.

Jason Momoa is just Jason Momoa! He is like a tidal wave of Jason every time he walks into a room, and I mean that in a good way. He's just this wonderful character who's full of life and energy, and incredible strength and power. What he brings

01 Henry Cavill on set

02 London mourns for Superman

03 An early Superman concept sketch

04 Superman in full costume

05 Superman's eternal flame

06 A mysterious message on Superman's monument

to Aquaman is something which I know people are ready for. He really brings a special quality to it. And Ezra Miller as The Flash – I never even questioned the way he plays it. It's really, really well done. I think he's probably going to be a lot of people's favorite character in this movie.

What kind of physical preparation have you had to do for the role?
I did an awful lot to physically prepare. My trainer, Michael Blevins, took me through five months of the usual stuff, which is a mass gain period. I got up to about 220 pounds. Then we started slowly shaving off the calories as the workload increased, and then held

> **"**
> # THIS IS THE FIRST TIME WE SEE THE TRUE SUPERMAN... THE SUPERMAN WHO IS CONFIDENT, AND SURE, AND FULL OF HOPE AND JOY.
> **"**

the workload and started taking off the calories even more. It was five months of grind, but it was always enjoyable as much as it was a challenge.

How did you enjoy being on set at Leavesden Studios in the UK?
It's great being here, you know. It's nice working from home. The energy here is really, really good. There's a real positivity around. It's good fun, and it's great to have more heroes around.

We also have the Kent farm, all the way over here in England. They're doing some very clever effects stuff, where it's going to look like we were actually in the same place that we shot the original Kent farm (for *Man of Steel*). It feels and looks exactly like the original Kent farm, but it's a lot colder because we're here in England rather than Illinois.

How does it feel to play such an iconic character?
There's nothing quite like playing Superman. It's something which I

01

03

GYM BUDDIES

***Justice League Collector's Edition*: Did the *Justice League* cast spend much time together in preparation for this movie?**
Henry Cavill: "The most time we see each other, apart from actually being on set, is probably in the gym. There are lots of crossovers in the gym where we're sitting there supporting each other, whether we are training with each other or separately. The guys have been fantastic, they really have. They have worked extraordinarily hard to get into incredible shape for this movie, as you guys will see."

am thankful for every day. I know it sounds silly when I say that, but I'm being honest. I get excited about it still. My friends and I talk about it; we geek out about Superman, and I have this moment where I forget that I'm actually the guy who is playing the character! I get to represent this incredibly important character in the movie world, at this period in time, and for me that's an honor and a mantle I gladly bear. ◖

THE COMIC BOOK ORIGINS OF...
CLARK KENT/KAL-EL — SUPERMAN

FEATURE BY NICK JONES

REAL NAME CLARK KENT/KAL-EL

CREATED BY JERRY SIEGEL AND JOE SHUSTER

FIRST APPEARANCE *ACTION COMICS* #1 (JUNE 1938)

FIRST JOINED THE LEAGUE *BRAVE AND THE BOLD* (VOL. 1) #28 (MARCH 1960)

POWER AND ABILITIES FUELED BY EARTH'S YELLOW SUN, SUPERMAN POSSESSES SUPERHUMAN STRENGTH AND SPEED, ALONG WITH INVULNERABILITY AND THE POWER OF FLIGHT. OTHER ABILITIES INCLUDE X-RAY AND HEAT VISION, FREEZE BREATH, AND SUPER-HEARING.

It's an enduring irony that the greatest hero the world has ever known doesn't actually hail from this planet. And yet Superman has become Earth's primary protector, fighting a never-ending battle for truth and justice – a symbol of hope, both for mankind and for the Justice League.

Few can be unaware of Superman's origin: how the baby Kal-El was rocketed from the doomed planet Krypton as a baby; how he was raised by kindly farmers Jonathan and Martha Kent as their son, Clark; how, as he grew up in the Kansas town of Smallville, Earth's yellow sun and relatively low gravity granted him incredible powers; how he became a reporter for the *Daily Planet* in Metropolis, and donned a colorful costume to battle evil as Superman, the Man of Steel. What's surprising is that a good many of those elements weren't present in Superman's origin in his first appearance in *Action Comics* #1 – no mention of "Kal-El" or naming of Krypton; no Ma and Pa Kent or Smallville; and the *Daily Planet* was the *Daily Star*. Even so, the core elements that would come to define Superman were established, including the dynamic between Clark/Superman and his newspaper colleague, love interest, and eventual wife, Lois Lane.

Within a few years, the legend of Superman would be embellished to

include additional powers like flight (at first, Superman could merely "hurdle a 20-story building"), X-ray vision, and heat vision, as well as such staples as Jimmy Olsen (who, after an unnamed cameo in *Action Comics* #6 in 1938, made his first full appearance in *Superman* #13 in 1941), Lex Luthor (who debuted in *Action Comics* #23 in 1940), and Kryptonite – not to mention,

through the 1950s and into the 1960s, an entire menagerie of super-powered pets and animals (including Krypto and Beppo the Super-Monkey!).

When the Justice League came into being in *Brave and the Bold* #28, it was natural that Superman should be a central part of the team, but as the world's most powerful hero, the competing demands for his attention

04

05

were evident from the get-go. When, in that debut League story, the signal went out for the team to assemble and combat Starro the Conqueror, Superman was forced to demur, as he was already in deep space saving the Earth from a shower of giant meteors. Nevertheless, Superman would come to be seen as inseparable from the Justice League, his selfless heroism a constant inspiration, his absence keenly felt when he wasn't on the team.

Over the years Superman's cast and mythos expanded – adding enemies like Brainiac, allies such as his cousin, Supergirl, and world-building elements like the Fortress of Solitude – while his powers waxed and waned, depending on the whims of the creators at the time. Then, in 1986, in the wake of the previous year's alternate reality-destroying crossover event *Crisis on Infinite Earths*, Superman was reinvented for the modern age by writer/artist John Byrne in the *Man of Steel* mini-series. (Just prior to

it, writer Alan Moore and artist Curt Swan brought the preceding 50 years to a close with the classic two-part story "Whatever Happened to the Man of Tomorrow?") Each issue of Byrne's series focused on a different era of Superman's life, retelling and reimagining his origin in the first installment, before depicting his arrival in Metropolis and first meeting with Lois Lane, encountering Batman for the first time, and so forth.

Byrne's take on Superman essentially served as the template for the Man of Steel for pretty much the next 20 years. Which isn't to say those years were uneventful…

In 1993, Superman made headlines in the real world when he was killed by the monstrous Doomsday in the "Death of Superman" storyline. Succeeding issues of the various Superman titles saw a variety of candidates jostling to replace him in "Rise of the Supermen!", before Superman himself made a triumphant return. Soon after, Clark and

01
Superman versus the dreaded Doomsday

02
Superman reinvented in John Byrne's *Man of Steel* #1

03
The "New 52" era ends – and the "Rebirth" era begins…

04
Superman debuts in 1938's *Action Comics* #1

05
Superman gets his own title in 1939

Lois married, and Superman assumed a more prominent role in the Justice League – after a lengthy absence from the roster – in the 1997-launched *JLA*.

In 2003, elements of Superman's origin were again revised in the *Birthright* mini-series, and again in 2009 in the *Superman: Secret Origin* miniseries. However, within a few short years a more radical overhaul would take place. As part of the 2011 DC Comics "New 52" initiative, aspects of Superman's history were altered – notably his initial arrival in Metropolis, where he was depicted wearing a makeshift costume comprising T-shirt and jeans, and his relationship with Lois, which remained platonic. When that Superman died in 2016, he was replaced by his forebear for a time, until the two versions of Superman were merged, restoring much of Clark's history, including not only his marriage to Lois, but the son they had together, Jon, alias the new Superboy. ◼

01

BIO

Jonathan Kimble **Simmons** was born in Grosse Pointe, Michigan. To date, he has appeared in 76 films, 67 TV series, six stage plays, and he has supplied his vocal talents for six video games, including *Portal 2*. His most memorable roles include *Peter Pan* (as Captain Hook), *Guys and Dolls, Law and Order, Homicide: Life on the Streets, Spin City, Oz, Zootopia, Juno, The Simpsons*, and Sam Raimi's *Spider-Man* trilogy, where he played J. Jonah Jameson. He has won numerous awards for his performance in the 2014 film *Whiplash* – including an Academy Award, a Golden Globe, and a BAFTA for Best Supporting Actor.

J.K. SIMMONS
COMMISSIONER GORDON

J.K. Simmons has made a huge impact on the big and small screens over the last few decades, and now he gets to take on a hugely iconic character, Commissioner Gordon. How has he approached the role, how does he perceive Gordon, and also, what prop would he steal from the set...?

Justice League Collector's Edition: Did you have a favorite DC character when you were growing up?
J.K. Simmons: Growing up, my favorite was Superman. I probably should say Batman, shouldn't I?

What excites you about being part of this project?
Being a part of this iconic world is a brilliant thing for any actor. To be the latest actor to play Commissioner Gordon is a real honor.

Who is Commissioner Gordon in your view?
My take on Commissioner Gordon is that he's a badass. But that's an under-appreciated part of who he is,

because he's eclipsed by the ultimate badass, Batman.

But Gordon is a tough ex-Marine, who worked his way up and can handle himself in the turf of bad guys. Compared to Batman, he's just a regular guy, but compared to most people, he's a champion.

You keep fit – did you want that for this character?
I've been just trying to fight Father Time and stay fit for the last several years. It does work well with the character, but I haven't been specifically getting fit just for it – it's for general life.

How did the filmmakers approach you for this project?

02

What does Gordon think about vigilante justice?

There are two sides to the whole concept of vigilantism. Commissioner Gordon recognizes the importance of it but it's not something that the officials in power are gonna be big fans of. Gotham is kind of a mess in just about every way.

There are many iconic elements in the film – the Bat-Signal, the rooftops of Gotham… How do you feel acting in scenes involving them?

Being on the rooftop and turning on the Bat-Signal have been really iconic moments for me. I know they will be for the fans as well. When you're working, it's just another shot in another day and you approach it all like a professional and just try to live in the moment. But, there's no denying that there's a certain kind of buzz to it. It's surrounded by green screens but there's enough reality to create the environment. It's one of those boyhood fantasy things come true.

Gotham is almost a character, isn't it? How is it portrayed in this film?

It's a bit of a downtrodden, haggard character; a little ragged, a little beaten down. Maybe that's why they selected me to play Commissioner Gordon!

Why do you think the DC characters have a big universal appeal and enduring popularity?

I think the DC Universe and this kind of movie have a great international appeal. They're universal characters who people can relate to. Batman specifically is the dark, brooding version of the reluctant Super Hero. And in fact, he's not even a Super Hero, he's just a hero. He's just a guy who has worked very hard for what he believes in.

Finally, are there any props you want to take home with you?

No, I haven't stolen anything from the set… but I haven't finished filming, so we'll see… Maybe I'll grab Gordon's mustache. Funny thing about that – when I first started shooting, I'd kept wearing a mustache for the previous character I played, so it was perfect. Then I had to shave it off for another job in-between shoots. So the fans will have to be on the lookout for the scene with Gordon wearing a fake mustache… I'm guessing they won't be able to tell. ◗

These things are top secret because everybody wants to find out all the information about these big movies ahead of time. I don't understand it! For me it just spoils the fun of seeing the movie. But because it's so top secret, I got a call from my agent saying that several high-profile members of a film's team wanted to meet with me, though he didn't know what the project was at the time. So I went along, and 20 minutes into the conversation I said, "I have absolutely no idea what you're talking about." Then there was this moment of, "Oh right, nobody's allowed to know anything – so, let's fill you in…"

Did you have any assumptions?

I thought maybe they wanted me to play a new bad guy. When Jim Gordon's name came into the mix, I was thrilled.

Did you do any research into the character?

Most kids don't grow up thinking, "Gee, I wish I was Commissioner Gordon." You grow up wanting to be Batman or Superman. I did a little research mostly with two friends of mine who are huge DC fans. I got some of their valued opinions and did some reading. I didn't do any specific police research as I had done that for many films in the past.

01
Commissioner Gordon prepares to meet a Dark figure

02
Simmons/Gordon at work at the Gotham Police Station

03
J.K. Simmons as Commissioner Gordon

04
Batman and Commissioner Gordon

AMY ADAMS
LOIS LANE

After the death of Superman in *Batman v Superman*, Lois Lane has had to rediscover her role at *The Daily Planet* as well as find her place in a strange new world... Actress Amy Adams discusses Lois' role in *Justice League*...

BIO

Born in Vicenza, Italy, **Amy Adams** is an award-winning actress. Raised in Colorado, Adams began her career in dance and theater before moving to LA in 1999. She landed a major role in 2002's *Catch Me if You Can*, before securing her breakout role as the princess Giselle in 2007's *Enchanted*, which earned her a Golden Globe nomination for Best Actress in a Motion Picture Musical or Comedy. Recently, she played Lois Lane in *Man of Steel* (2013) and con-artist Sydney Prosser in *American Hustle* (2014). In 2016, she starred in the critically acclaimed *Arrival*, and reprised her role as Lois in *Batman v Superman*.

Justice League Collector's Edition: Have you been keeping up to date with Lois Lane's stories in the comic books?

Amy Adams: A little bit, yeah. My husband is really into comics and any time I have a question, he refers to Lois' canon and how to bring truth to her and what she's going through now. I've been corrected quite a bit!

How would you describe Lois in Justice League?

What I like about Lois is that the girl's really gone through a lot! She's gone through a lot in the canon, as have all the characters. It really gives you permission to put your own stamp on it.

How is she coping?

She has been isolated writing puff pieces for the *Daily Planet*. She'd been feeling that she couldn't go back and face the world just yet.

What about Martha Kent – Clark's adopted mother? What is Lois and Martha's relationship like now?

Martha is still about family and love. She has that great maternal strength that I think everybody needs in their life. Martha offers that strength to Lois the same way that she did to Clark, so she's really taken her on as her own.

What is it like coming back?

Not only do I get to come back and rejoin the cast – which is always fun – but there's a whole crew I have worked with now for six or seven years. From the first person I see in the morning to the last person I see at night, there's always someone there that I know. It feels like a family and you really feel that bond and that sense of unity of all being in it together.

Do you think the fans are going to freak out when they see the movie?

Oh my gosh, I freaked out about the costumes. The way that the characters have been interpreted is so cool. I feel cool being in the movies, so that's good because I'm not cool... I'm cool like a 90-year-old woman is cool!

How are the actors looking in their costumes and as the characters?

I've seen some footage. I love Ezra Miller's sensibility and the humor that he brings to The Flash. I've seen everybody walking around in different states of their costumes and it's pretty amazing.

What about Jason Momoa as Aquaman?

Aquaman in the comics has been in tights, and that is not how they've presented this Aquaman. He looks very dominating and very strong, and you can really imagine him ruling the ocean. There's something primal about Jason as Aquaman.

> **WHAT I LIKE ABOUT LOIS IS THAT THE GIRL'S REALLY GONE THROUGH A LOT — AS HAVE ALL THE CHARACTERS.**

POLICE LINE - DO NOT CRO
METROPOLIS POLICE DEPT.

How is Ray looking as Cyborg?
I have not seen him in his costume, but I know he works out really hard. I have to say, all of the main actors work out so hard. They train so rigorously to achieve these physiques. They make it look easy, but I know how hard they work. I look forward to seeing how the film comes together.

And how about Gal Gadot as Wonder Woman?
Seeing her in the costume is completely awesome, and I'm so glad she exists and that the world of the

01
Amy Adams on the *Daily Planet* set as Lois Lane with Diane Lane as Martha Kent

02
Lois faces up to the tragedies of *Batman v Superman*

03
Behind the scenes with Lois reflecting at Heroes Park and the Superman statue

04
Lois is well and truly back in action in *Justice League*

Amazons exists for my daughter to emulate. It's really, really cool.

How has it been to see women become more a part of these Super Hero franchises?
I like that they're bringing in these strong female characters that offer more than just a foil to the men. I think that's really important for young girls to see, and to see how they can exist in a world with men, but not exist *for* men. That's really important for me to show my daughter. And it's important for men

to see as well, because that's not how it is in the world. It's nice to see it reflected in film.

Was there a moment when you walked onto the set and you thought, "that is so cool!"?
What's amazing to me is the world that the special effects department creates. I only see a small portion, but what I see is amazing: the live sets they built are so detailed. I have so much respect for the visual effects and sound effects teams. They're so good and I don't know how they do it. I'm very appreciative because they make it all come together in a way I would not be able to imagine. Using practical elements when they can creates a sense of reality in this super-real world. ◗

JEREMY IRONS
ALFRED PENNYWORTH

BIO

Born in Cowes on the Isle of Wight, **Jeremy Irons** began his acting career on stage in 1969 before moving to film in 1980. In 1981, he was nominated by BAFTA for a Best Actor award for his first major film role in *The French Lieutenant's Woman*. In 1991, he won an Oscar for Best Actor in *Reversal of Fortune*. Irons' career has expanded across various iconic films over the years, including *Die Hard with a Vengeance*, *High-Rise*, and *Assassin's Creed*. His first appearance as Alfred Pennyworth was in *Batman v Superman: Dawn of Justice*.

Alfred has always been there for Bruce Wayne and Batman – but how will that dynamic change when the Dark Knight gets a whole new group of costumed friends? Actor Jeremy Irons discusses Alfred's new challenges in *Justice League*…

Justice League Collector's Edition: What is the essence of the *Justice League* story from Alfred's perspective?
Jeremy Irons: It's about Alfred's boss, Bruce Wayne, trying to get a team together to fight what he has to fight. Alfred and Bruce haven't talked much about it, but Bruce has spent a lot of time trying to pull this team together – this league of heroes. Alfred goes along with it as he thinks Mr Wayne probably knows best, but Alfred is not sure how much of a team builder or team player Bruce is. Time will tell…

When Bruce brings the rest of the team together, does Alfred have that same sense of loyalty to them?
Alfred doesn't know much about them. He just welcomes them into the cave and makes them tea – he had to find extra cups! He thinks the League are a strange lot. Alfred's role is to take care of Bruce, and Alfred hopes that this team will also take care of Bruce.

What do you think the audience will most like about the *Justice League* story?
I think they will enjoy the fact that we get to meet such interesting and colorful heroes. They will enjoy their quirks – not only in the way they dress, but in what they can do, and how they are in their "hidden life." They have character, they have individuality, and we'll get to see what they can do together.

And the Batmobile is updated for this film?
There are a few updates, yes. A cannon here, some machines there, and of course a rocket launcher in the front. Typical Bruce to remove the co-pilot chair to make room for a large cannon! Alfred keeps busy mechanically and electronically and comes up with the odd thing – the odd surprise – for Bruce.

It seems like Batman can only get into a vehicle that opens with the doors swinging upwards…?
I think he tends to prefer gull wing doors. It's something to do with not

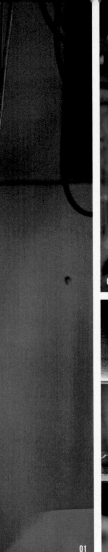

01
Jeremy Irons
prepares for DC
action again as
Alfred Pennyworth

02
Jeremy Irons with
Gal Gadot as Diana
Prince/Wonder
Woman in the Bat
Hangar set

03
Alfred travels in style

04
Alfred and Bruce
with the upgraded
Batmobile

05
Alfred tinkers with
another invention

wanting to bang his head! As you get older, it's easier if you can have something that comes up so you can get in and then sit down, rather than trying to get in sideways. He's quite a big Super Hero!

What's Alfred's relationship to Diana?
Well, I have to say that she bucks the place up a bit. Two blokes together is fine, but when Diana comes around, she does cheer the place up (*chuckles*)! Alfred is always very pleased when she's there. We don't talk a lot because she's quite a focused individual, but I like to think Alfred is able to broaden her life a little bit. He can teach her how to make a proper cup of tea, which may not seem important in the larger scheme of things – but God is in the details, and I think one of those details is how to make a really nice English cup of tea!

All the kids who visited the set seem to want an Alfred!
Well, don't we all want an Alfred? I would love an Alfred. Someone who is uncomplaining, who keeps

> **GOD IS IN THE DETAILS, AND I THINK ONE OF THOSE DETAILS IS HOW TO MAKE A REALLY NICE ENGLISH CUP OF TEA!**

the vehicles running, keeps the lawnmower sharp, chops the wood, keeps the fire going, does a bit of cooking... He always seems to be there and he is ready and willing. He's a dream. He's not a Super Hero, but I think he could be regarded as a bit of a hero.

Are you ever surprised at the way kids react to these types of characters?
It's strange because they know you are an actor, and yet you embody this

person who's enormous on a screen. I suppose the first time this happens for children is with Father Christmas.

I'm delighted that so many generations – not just children – are quite taken with these stories and these characters. It's lovely to be part of that fictional universe. 🔳

JOE MORTON

SILAS STONE

In *Justice League*, we get to know more about the lives of the individual team members – including getting the chance to meet Cyborg's father, Silas Stone, played by award-winning actor Joe Morton. Here, Morton provides an insight into Silas' role...

01

Justice League Collector's Edition: Please introduce us to your character in *Justice League*...
Joe Morton: I'm playing Silas Stone, and he is the creator of Cyborg.

And your character is related to Cyborg too?
Yes, he's Silas' son. He was in a terrible accident. I steal this alien thing called a Mother Box, because I suspect that it might have some properties that are useful. I find out that it does and I use it to keep him alive, and basically change his physical being.

Do we always know what kind of monster we're creating?
Most of the time I think we do. Even in *Frankenstein* there was the idea that things could go awry because you have no idea what kind of personality its brain had. With *T2*, it was a chip that became a Terminator. I don't think Miles Dyson had any idea that's where it was going.

And with Cyborg, Silas is trying to teach his son that this is how he is going to look all the time. Cyborg now has a choice – he can still use who he is and what he is for good, instead of allowing it to make him bitter and angry.

You can't change your physical being, but you can still make it something that's positive and life-affirming.

Is Silas able to reconnect with his son in this movie?
Eventually, yes. Victor is coping with the loss of his mother and his transformation in his own way and

BIO

Joe Morton was born in Harlem, New York and made his acting debut on Broadway in the musical *Hair*. He went on to appear in *Salvation*, and *Raisin*, for which he was nominated for a Tony Award. Since his first lead role in the 1984 movie *Brother from Another Planet*, directed by John Sayles, Morton has gone on to appear in many films including *Terminator 2: Judgment Day* – in which he played Dr. Miles Bennett Dyson, the creator of Skynet – *Speed*, *Apt Pupil*, *Of Mice and Men*, *Executive Decision*, *Ali*, and *American Gangster*. On TV he has appeared in *M*A*S*H*, *Smallville*, *Eureka*, and *Scandal*, for which he won an Emmy Award for Outstanding Guest Actor in a Drama Series.

it takes both characters an immense amount of personal growth through the film to begin the discussion of reconnecting.

Do you know about the DC canon and the DC world? Did you grow up with the comics?
I didn't. My father was in the Army and his job was to integrate the Armed Forces overseas, which usually meant that we arrived at a post unannounced. And once they realized who he was and what he was doing, his life became very difficult – our lives became very difficult. So comics weren't really on my radar.

The only comic books I ended up reading were the "classic comics" like *A Tale of Two Cities*, and that kind of thing.

Did you ever watch *Wonder Woman* or *Batman* on TV?
I think I did when I was a kid. We were in Germany and Japan and those kind of places, and there was *Superman* and all of that on television. By the time I got to high school, maybe *Superman* was still on TV, so I saw a little bit of that. I started watching more movies than television once I got older. ■

03

01
Silas tries to discover the secrets of the Mother Box

02
Joe takes a break from his dramatic role

03
Morton with Ray Fisher, who plays his on-screen son, Victor

04
Silas Stone as played by Joe Morton

> " SILAS IS TRYING TO TEACH HIS SON THAT THIS IS HOW HE IS GOING TO LOOK ALL THE TIME — AND THAT CYBORG CAN STILL USE WHO HE IS AND WHAT HE IS FOR GOOD, INSTEAD OF ALLOWING IT TO MAKE HIM BITTER AND ANGRY. "

CIARÁN HINDS
STEPPENWOLF

Ciarán Hinds has appeared in many TV, movie, and theater productions – but you've never seen him like this! Hinds plays Steppenwolf, a monstrous, fully computer-generated character in *Justice League*. He joins us – in human form – to reveal all about the role...

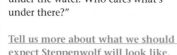

02

Justice League Collector's Edition: Who is Steppenwolf?
Ciarán Hinds: I guess you'd call him a super-villain. He hails from the planet of Apokolips and he is the general of the Apokoliptian army who has come to take the world. For thousands of years he's been in search of the Mother Boxes, which are all-powerful entities. He's in search of all-power, and that's his journey.

Do you not want him to get that power?
I suppose nobody wants him to get that, do they? Nobody wants anybody to get that, frankly.

What are Steppenwolf's powers?
His powers are physical rather than any form of mental agility. His real powers are wielded through his extraordinary axe weapon. When he chooses to use it, it creates mayhem and it decimates everything around it.

And Steppenwolf travels around through a "Boom Tube"?
Yes – it's like a transporter, or a super shuttle that goes between universes. It transports people quickly from another place and places them in a certain location.

What is his history with humans, Amazons, and Atlanteans?
The Mother Boxes. There's one under the sea with the Atlanteans, there's one in the hands of the Amazons, and one with mankind. They don't even know what's inside of it, they just know it's protected and must never get out of their hands.

How does he feel about the Atlanteans?
He couldn't give a toss about the Atlanteans! He thinks, "keep them under the water. Who cares what's under there?"

Tell us more about what we should expect Steppenwolf will look like.

BIO

Born in Belfast, Northern Ireland, **Ciarán Hinds** began his acting career in a 1976 stage production of *Cinderella*. He went on to appear in the TV series *Rome* (as Gaius Julius Caesar), *Above Suspicion*, and the Emmy Award-winning *Game of Thrones*. He made his film debut in 1981's *Excalibur* and went on to appear in *Road to Perdition*, *The Sum of All Fears*, *Munich*, *There Will Be Blood*, *Harry Potter and the Deathly Hallows Part 2*, *The Woman in Black*, *Tinker Tailor Soldier Spy*, *Ghost Rider: Spirit of Vengeance*, and *Frozen*. He has also enjoyed extended runs with the Royal Shakespeare Company, The Royal National Theatre and Glasgow's Citizens Theatre.

Basically, you'll see this rather impressive figure, about 8 feet tall, almost like a Viking mixed with a Celt. You can tell this guy is a marauder.

Did you have to do any physical preparation for the action sequences?
No, because if I was using that axe, I probably wouldn't have got it off the ground. We used a much lighter axe, which you can swing through the air.

Steppenwolf clearly inspires a lot of fear in this film...
Steppenwolf is a frightening character, there's no doubt about it. As soon as you see him, you just know, "Holy God, here comes trouble." He is not a fearful man at all, because he believes he can handle anything. He wishes to create fear – not just that people should be afraid of him, but I think he gets pleasure out of it.

How did you go about approaching such a prominent, terrifying villain? You're not a scary man – where do you go inside yourself to find this?
Basically, I think awful thoughts and imagine how easy it would be to be in complete control, or to want complete control. And if there's

01

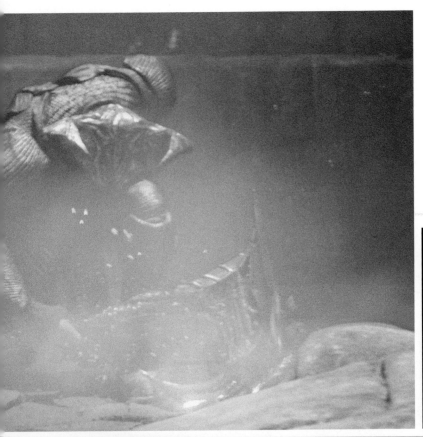

being a mechanical or digital process, they are able to observe and create from that.

Is that a challenge?
You have to use your imagination. You're in a room, a blank room with just a few dots, and you've got to imagine some people are there. You've got to point to, "oh that's… Hippolyta, and that's… Cyborg!" You've got to imagine them around you and then go to work with them.

Are these the first Super Heroes that your character has encountered?
If you come from the planet Apokolips we're all super beings – so Super Heroes are nothing. While the humans are looking around saying, "they're amazing," we're going, "pfft, whatever!" I think that's why Steppenwolf comes in with this assumed arrogance.

What does the Justice League mean to you personally?
The idea of togetherness or understanding when things are bad. People reaching out to say, "can anyone help here? Who do you need?" To actually reach out and bring some light into the situation. To be quite honest, that's as big a task as you can get. 🛡

anything in my way, what's the best way to remove it…

Did you read any comic books before?
I grew up in the north of Ireland in the '50s and '60s. The comic world never came to me. So, I'd say my first contact with the comic world was the first *Superman* film with Christopher Reeve. I saw it when I was in my early 20s and I felt it had a real kind of magic about it.

Do you have a favorite Super Hero?
I quite like The Flash! He makes

me laugh because he's just like a little kid. What's great about these Super Hero stories is there's a human side to them – that's what makes them connect.

Today you did some mocap. What does that entail?
Motion capture, or "mocap," is when a helmet is placed onto your head with two very fine cameras. The cameras capture your face, so they can then transpose it onto the character of Steppenwolf, digitally. They also have other cameras at the side that capture my natural movement. Rather than it

01
Steppenwolf in attack mode

02
Steppenwolf makes his explosive entrance

03
Early concept art for the *Justice League* movie's main villain

04
Concept painting of Steppenwolf with a Mother Box (uh-oh…)

05
Steppenwolf, as brought to life in the film by Ciarán Hinds

THE COMIC BOOK ORIGINS OF...
THE JUSTICE LEAGUE

I ndividually, they are the strongest, bravest, swiftest, boldest, smartest heroes in the DC Universe, each possessed of incredible powers, fearsome intellects, or astonishing technology or weaponry (or even a combination of all those things). Together, they are more than the sum of their parts, united against the direst threats to humanity. They are the World's Greatest Super Heroes: the Justice League.

There had been teams of masked men (and women) in comic books before the advent of the Justice League – notably the Justice Society of America – but the League was something else entirely – a brilliant but simple notion: a group composed of DC's biggest, most powerful heroes, battling science-fictional villains and monsters rather than the traditional Nazis, spies, and saboteurs. The idea for a new super-team had its genesis in DC Comics editor Julius Schwartz, who had revamped a succession of the company's World War II-era "Golden Age" heroes – The Flash (Jay Garrick), Green Lantern (Alan Scott), Hawkman (Carter Hall), and The Atom (Al Pratt) – into new versions through the 1950s and into the early 1960s, kickstarting the "Silver Age" of comics. Building on this success, Schwartz hit on the notion of an update of the first super-team, the Justice Society, whose wartime exploits had featured, among others, Doctor Fate, Hour-Man, and the Spectre, along with the aforementioned

Flash, Green Lantern, Hawkman, and Atom. Schwartz assigned writer Gardner Fox (co-creator of the Justice Society) and artist Mike Sekowsy. The result was the Justice League of America: the revamped Green Lantern (Hal Jordan) and Flash (Barry Allen) alongside DC's original heroes Superman, Batman, Wonder Woman, and Aquaman, plus a relatively recent invention, the Martian Manhunter (J'onn J'onzz, who had debuted in 1955).

Tagged "The World's Greatest Heroes," the Justice League blasted into action in *The Brave and the Bold* #28, cover-dated March 1960, battling extraterrestrial invader Starro the Conqueror. Such sci-fi trappings were typical of the DC comics of the era (Schwartz had a background in science fiction fandom and had been a literary agent representing Ray Bradbury and Robert Bloch, while Fox had written for the SF pulp magazines), and set the tone for the League's adventures going forward. After tangling with far-future villain the Weapons Master, crazed inventor Professor Ivo, and super-powered android Amazo in the next two issues of *Brave and the Bold*, the League launched into their own series in November 1960.

The first issue of *Justice League of America* continued the sci-fi theme, pitting the team against extra-dimensional despot Despero. Following issues introduced space tyrant Kanjar Ro,

03

04

01
A team meeting in the Justice League's first appearance in 1960's *The Brave and the Bold* #28

02
The team head into action on the cover to 2011's *Justice League* #1

03
The cover to the JLA's first appearance in *The Brave and the Bold* #28

04
A fun cover from 1961's *Justice League of America* issue #7

evil scientist Doctor Destiny, and luck manipulator Amos Fortune (who would later lead playing card-themed criminals the Royal Flush Gang), all of whom would reappear to bedevil the League multiple times over ensuing decades. Aiding the League in these adventures was honorary team member Snapper Carr, a teenager who'd assisted the team against Starro and had since sat in whenever the League convened at their secret headquarters in Happy Harbor, Rhode Island, where Snapper lived.

Issue #9 of *Justice League of America* brought something that had heretofore been missing: an origin. Assembling at their headquarters to celebrate their third birthday as a team, one by one the Leaguers recounted to a rapt Snapper how they first came together. Seven powerful alien claimants to the throne of the planet Appellax had arrived on Earth, intending to turn it into a battleground on which they would fight for supremacy – using transformed humans as foot soldiers – until only one of them remained. Unable to best the Appellaxians individually, Superman, Batman, Wonder Woman, Aquaman, Green Lantern, The Flash, and the Martian Manhunter had joined forces to defeat the invaders, after which they had determined to form "a league against evil! Our purpose will be to uphold justice against whatever danger threatens it!"

As the series continued, further villains assailed the Justice League, including ancient sorcerer Felix Faust and master of photokinesis Doctor Light. The League also added new members to their roster: Green Arrow (Oliver Queen), The Atom, (Ray Palmer), and Hawkman (Katar Hol from the planet Thanagar).

Then, in issue #21, came the remarkable "Crisis on Earth One!" Prefigured by stories in The Flash's own

title where Barry Allen had met not only his Golden Age forebear, Jay Garrick, but the rest of the Justice Society, the Justice League reached across the gulf separating realities and summoned the Justice Society to their Earth (Earth-One), while they traveled to the JSA's Earth (Earth-Two) – each team in pursuit of their own foes. Not only was it the first of many team-ups between the two teams, but the story laid the groundwork for what would become the DC multiverse – myriad alternate realities.

In *Justice League of America* #29, the League faced a team of villains from Earth-Three who were both strikingly familiar and alarmingly strange. The Crime Syndicate of America comprised five evil analogs of core Leaguers: Ultraman, Superwoman, Owlman, Power Ring, and Johnny Quick, who launched devastating assaults on both Earth-One and the home of the Justice Society, Earth-Two. They were defeated in the following issue, but would return to repeatedly plague the League.

As a new decade neared, the Justice League began to change – as did their creators. Artist Mike Sekowsy and writer Fox both left the series toward the end of the 1960s. Stepping into their shoes were artist Dick Dillin and successive

05
A new roster is created in 2006's *Justice League of America* #1

06
The team analyze a recent battle in *Justice League of America* #5 from 1961

07
Grant Morrison and Howard Porter relaunch the team's adventures in 1997's *JLA* #1

writers Denny O'Neil, Len Wein, and Steve Englehart (among others), and with them came a new era for the League. The team established a new headquarters in orbit around the Earth – the Justice League satellite. Accordingly, the threats became more cosmic in nature, while the League's roster expanded to include such heroes as Black Canary, Elongated Man, Red Tornado, sorcerer Zatanna, Hawkgirl (Hawkman's wife), Firestorm, and occasionally The Phantom Stranger.

The tone of the stories became edgier, notably when the Justice League was given a new origin in 1977's *Justice League of America* #144. Martian Manhunter revealed how years ago he had aided a group of heroes who had banded together to stop an invasion of White Martians, his sworn enemies. After defeating the invaders, the heroes decided to form "A league against evil," but realizing that the public would not accept a Martian on the team, they did not announce their formation until months later, after the Appellaxian invasion.

Another significant tale from this era saw the League again teaming up with the Justice Society as the two teams encountered the New Gods. In *Justice League of America* #183–185, members

WITHHOLDING HIS ANSWERS WHILE THE OTHERS TAKE *DOCTOR DESTINY* AND HIS MEN TO POLICE HEADQUARTERS, THE *GREEN GLADIATOR* SPEEDS AWAY TO RECHARGE HIS *POWER RING*, THEN JOINS HIS FELLOW-MEMBERS AT THE SECRET SANCTUARY...

CAUGHT BY HIS WILL-DEADENING BEAM, I WAS PLACED ON ONE OF THOSE PLATFORMS, WHERE I OVERHEARD *DOCTOR DESTINY'S* MEN TALKING! THUS I LEARNED OF HIS PLAN TO CAPTURE YOU ALL...

08
A brand new era in 2016's *Justice League: Rebirth #1*

09 (clockwise from top left): Different realities meet in 1963's *Justice League of America #21*; the Justice League and the Justice Society of America fight side by side in *Justice League of America #22*; a new (slightly funnier) beginning in 1987's *Justice League* – the series would later be known as *Justice League International*; the team is reborn in the 1980s mini-series, *Legends*

of both teams were abducted and transported to New Genesis, home of the New Gods, to assist in a conflict between that planet and its dark twin, Apokolips.

Change had been a feature of the Justice League since the team's earliest days, but in the 1980s, the changes became ever more stark. A war between Earth and Mars saw the Justice League satellite destroyed, and with most of the core members all absent from the roster, Aquaman elected to disband the League and create a new one. Incorporating a number of street-level heroes, this version of the team set up shop in Detroit. A year later, the League was shaken by even bigger changes, first by the reality-reordering epic *Crisis on Infinite Earths*, during which The Flash was killed and myriad alternate Earths were destroyed, then by the crossover *Legends*, during which the League itself disbanded.

At the close of *Legends*, realizing that a brotherhood of heroes was needed now more than ever, Batman, Martian Manhunter, Doctor Fate, replacement Green Lantern Guy Gardner, Black Canary, Captain Marvel (alias Shazam), and Blue Beetle agreed to form a new Justice League. Launched into a new series by writer/artist team Keith Giffen, J.M. DeMatteis, and Kevin Maguire in 1987, this was a witty, anarchic take on the League, and the team transformed into Justice League International.

A relaunch came in 1997, under the guiding hands of writer Grant Morrison and artist Howard Porter. This retitled series, *JLA*, saw the "Big Seven" – Superman, Batman, Wonder Woman, Aquaman, Martian Manhunter,

The Flash (Wally West, the former Kid Flash), and Green Lantern (alias Kyle Rayner, who had replaced the then-dead Hal Jordan) – take center stage in a succession of epic storylines.

Through the 2000s, the Justice League was buffeted by a series of escalating crises: a murder mystery and hidden secrets in *Identity Crisis* (2004); the return of the multiverse in *Infinite Crisis* (2005); and the return of Barry Allen in *Final Crisis* (2008). But the most far-reaching crisis came in 2011, when the Flash-starring *Flashpoint* event rewrote the entire history of the DC Universe, not least that of the Justice League… As detailed by writer Geoff Johns and artist Jim Lee in 2011's relaunched *Justice League* series – part of a line-wide reboot by DC titled the "New 52" (later revisited and rechristened as "Rebirth") – it transpired that not only had the League been brought together under different circumstances than those described in the 1960s, but its founding members now included a character who hadn't even been invented back then: Cyborg.

Cyborg was placed front and center at the formation of the League, as, in a reimagined origin, the World's Greatest Super Heroes came together for the first time to fight an invasion by the forces of Apokolips and legions of Parademons. Cyborg's cybernetic systems allowing him to interface with the Apokoliptian technological marvels known as Mother Boxes, Cyborg played a decisive role in this battle, establishing his position as a key component in this reinvigorated, reenergized Justice League for the modern age. ■

OUTTAKES

To finish this publication, we have a special selection of funny, interesting, and unique images from shooting on the *Justice League* movie – we couldn't resist sharing them with you!

01
Gal Gadot having fun with Diana's Mercedes!

02
Hippolyta, Queen of the Amazons, and her loyal steed

03
Batman tries out a new weapon

04
Joe Morton and Ray Fisher play around on set

05
Gal Gadot plays charades – can you guess which Super Hero she's hinting at?

06
Jason Momoa makes a splash on location in Iceland

07
Ezra Miller limbers up on set with some yoga

08
Fun times on set with Ezra Miller and Gal Gadot

09
Gal Gadot with some li'l extras during filming of the Old Bailey scenes

OTHER GREAT TIE-IN COMPANIONS FROM TITAN
ON SALE NOW!

Rogue One – The Official Mission Debrief
ISBN 9781785861581

Rogue One – The Official Collector's Edition
ISBN 9781785861574

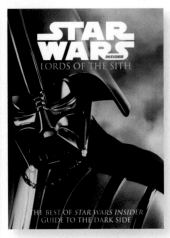

Star Wars: Lords of the Sith
ISBN 9781785851919

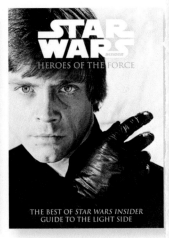

Star Wars: Heroes of the Force
ISBN 9781785851926

The Best of Star Wars Insider Volume 1
ISBN 9781785851162

The Best of Star Wars Insider Volume 2
ISBN 9781785851179

The Best of Star Wars Insider Volume 3
ISBN 9781785851896

The Best of Star Wars Insider Volume 4
ISBN 9781785851902

Star Trek: The Movies
ISBN 9781785855924

Fifty Years of Star Trek
ISBN 9781785855931

Star Trek – A Next Generation Companion
ISBN 9781785855948

Alien Covenant: The Official Collector's Edition
ISBN 9781785861925

TITANCOMICS
For more information visit www.titan-comics.com